What I *Really* Want to Do . . .

What I *Really* Want to Do . . .

How to Discover
The Right Job

Christopher Chamberlin Moore

CBP Press
St. Louis, Missouri

Unless otherwise indicated, all scripture quotations are from the Revised Standard Version of the Bible, copyrighted 1946, 1952, © 1971, 1973 by the Division of Christian Education of the National Council of Churches of Christ in America.

Library of Congress Cataloging in Publication Data

Moore, Christopher Chamberlin.
    What I really want to do— : how to discover the right job / Christopher Chamberlin Moore.
    140 p.   cm.
    Bibliography: p. 135.
    ISBN 0-8272-4226-3
    1. Vocational guidance. 2. Vocational interests. 3. Job hunting. I. Title.
HF5381.M673 1989
650. 1'4—dc 19   89-31291
                           CIP

Printed in the United States of America

Second printing

To Janice,
who listened,
and to
Alice and Douglas,
who will find
their own vocations

Contents

Part One: You and Your Job

Part Two: Five Steps to Career Satisfaction and Success

Chapter Four: Step Two—Have Some Crazy Dreams

Exercises to help you decide what you like to do. "Detective in my house." "My greatest achievement." "Letter to a friend." "Green with envy." Others. Translating crazy dreams into the requirements of a real job.

Chapter Five: Step Three—Focus on a Goal

The importance of a goal statement. Identifying occupations that correspond to your goal. Informational interviews. How to identify what is holding you back.

Chapter Six: Step Four—Assess Your Qualifications

The four qualifications for any job: skills qualifications; "paper" qualifications; experience qualifications; temperamental qualifications. Seeing your qualifications through the eyes of an employer. How to get qualifications when you don't have them.

Chapter Seven: Step Five—Go for It!

Four ways to change your occupational goal: job restructuring; job or career change; self-employment; getting started through volunteering. Identifying the strategies that will work best for you.

Part Three: Practical Strategies That Make a Difference

Part Four: Epilogue

Preface

Everyone has a dream.

For one it is starting a business. For another, changing jobs or even careers. For still another, advancing in a present position. For all, the dream represents the very best of what they hope to accomplish in the world.

Tragically, most people never realize their dream. For one thing, many people are not sure exactly what their dream is. Others, who do know, lack the courage or the knowledge to put it into operation.

What I Really Want to Do . . . will help you clearly define what it is you really want to do and how you can get paid for doing it. It will help you discover your vocation, that particular path that God has set for you and in which you will find true fulfillment in your work. I would like to thank the people I interviewed for this book, individuals from a variety of occupations who so generously shared their lives with me. I would also like to thank those whom I have been privileged to have as students in my career discovery workshops, which I have conducted throughout the country. They have provided the "reality testing" for the ideas, concepts, and exercises contained in this book.

In the course of researching and writing *What I Really Want to Do . . .* I have been reinforced in my belief that there is a particular work that is suited to each person. I believe that you can get paid for doing what you like! I believe that to do this is to be an effective steward of the gifts that God has given you. Finally, I believe that there are proven methods for discovering what you want to do, and also particular strategies that have proven successful in translating personal dreams into paid employment in the real world.

If your dream is to earn your living doing what *you* want to do, in accordance with the gifts and abilities that God has given you, then I invite you to read on.

Christopher Chamberlin Moore
New Bedford, Massachusetts

Part One

You and Your Job

Chapter One

Job, Career, or Vocation?

Do you enjoy what you do for a living?

If given the opportunity, would you choose to do it again?

If you answered *no* to both questions—or if you answered with a qualified *yes*—then it is likely that you are part of an estimated 80 percent of the American work force that is either:

—*misemployed:* working at a job for which you are not suited.

—*underemployed:* working at a job well below the level of your abilities.[1]

In either case, it is likely that you are not making the best use of the abilities that God has given you.

Let's look at some real life examples of people who are having problems with their work.

Misemployed: Mark Weigel and Ron Johnson[2]

Mark is an energetic young man who is two years out of college. He is the marketing director of a small computer software firm on the West Coast. Mark majored in business in college because, as he told his friend, "That is where the jobs are." Mark's real love, however, is tinkering with mechanical things. Even as a child he loved to take things apart and put them back together. One thing you notice about Mark is that, except when he is on the job, he seldom talks about computer software or about marketing surveys. Instead, he talks about the antique cars he would like to restore. Mark is beginning to have mixed feelings about his job. At first Mark was proud that he was able to land a job right out of college, in business, especially in a hot field like computer software. Now he's not so sure. And his doubts are beginning to be reflected in the quality of his work.

Mark is one of millions of people who are *misemployed*. That is, they are working in the wrong field—for them. They are working in a field for which they do not have the basic interest, or aptitudes, or temperament. They have chosen the field they are in for a variety of good reasons—like Mark's, because "that's where the jobs are." But basically they are not suited for the work, and consequently, it doesn't work, not for them and not for their employer.

Mark is misemployed because he chose the wrong field entirely. Mark's next-door neighbor, Ron, is misemployed because he was promoted to a job for which he is not suited.

Ron is a brilliantly innovative manager in a thriving electronics firm. Last year Ron developed a training program for the company's sales staff that was so successful that, as a reward, Ron's boss put him in charge of running it. A year later, and Ron is miserable.

"Ron, you should be happy. He's letting you run your own program," his wife keeps telling him.

Ron thinks he should be happy, too. But he knows he isn't. And he doesn't know what's wrong with him.

What's wrong with Ron is the fact that his promotion robbed him of doing what he enjoys and does best, and that is designing training programs. The actual running of the program he would prefer to leave to someone else.

Ron is like thousands of people who are so good at what they do that they have been promoted out of doing it—into something for which they are less well suited. Ron is like the high school math teacher who is moved up to assistant vice-principal. He trades his classroom for an office as he "advances" in the system. But what if he's really suited for the classroom and not the administrator's office?

Underemployed: Alisha Williams

Alisha is a young black woman who works as a teacher's aide in a third-grade public school classroom. Alisha loves the contact with the children, but she is also frustrated. She is frustrated because it seems there is really no future in what she is doing. She is frustrated at her pay—barely minimum wage—while the head teacher earns a professional salary considerably more than double hers. Above all, she is frustrated at the menial nature of the tasks assigned to her.

Alisha's problem is that she is *underemployed*. Unlike Mike and Ron, Alisha is in the right work, but her abilities are greater than the job demands of her. Consequently, she feels frustrated and cheated. Like many people in the work force, Alisha lacks either the credentials or the confidence to allow her to be employed at the level of responsibility where her real abilities could be used. But until she acquires these and changes her job, she will continue to remain underemployed—and frustrated.

Unemployed: Jeff Sikorski

Jeff is a sheet metal worker at a large shipyard in the Midwest. Or at least he was until he got his third layoff notice a few months ago. Now he sits at home and wonders what he will do.

When Jeff was younger, he never thought that much about jobs or careers. He went into the service right after high school. After the service he got a job in the shipyard. The pay was good. It never occurred to him that, fifteen years later, his job—in fact, the whole industry—would start drying up. Now Jeff is thirty-four and he wonders, "What do I do now? Where else can I get a job?"

Jeff is typical of many individuals in the contemporary American work force who have never reflected deeply about what they wanted to do, and who have not acquired high-level career-related skills. Consequently, when a recession comes, their unskilled, semiskilled, or outdated jobs are often the first to go.

Job, Career, and Vocation

Mark, Ron, Alisha, and Jeff have one thing in common, and it is something they have in common with thousands of other people in our society. It is the fact that, for a variety of different reasons, they are unhappy in their work and consequently are not effectively expressing the gifts that God has given them.

The problem in talking about work is that people may be

referring to very different experiences when they use the word *work*. For one, work may simply mean a paycheck at the end of the month. For another, work is an activity that helps give meaning and purpose to life. In fact, when people talk about work, they may be referring to one of three different things.

A Job

A job is work at its simplest level. Somebody tells you what to do and pays you to do it. There may be a sense of self-satisfaction involved in doing it, or there may not be. The important thing is that there is a contract between employer and employed: You do the work, and I'll reward you for doing it.

A job is what people think of when they think about work.

But work can involve much more than this.

A Career

A career usually implies a series of jobs over a period of time. What makes this series of jobs a *career* is two things. One, there is some "common thread" running through all the jobs. This common thread may be the profession or industry in which the person works. One person spends his whole life teaching, another his whole life working in the building trades. The common thread may also be the person's use of particular *skills.* Wherever a particular person has worked, she has always been in sales, for example.

The common thread is one characteristic of a career, while the other is some kind of upward movement. A person with a career generally *advances*. He or she moves up in the organization. As individuals move up, they generally improve in the use of the skills they have used throughout their career.

Many people, even those who have been working for many years, do not have a career. They have simply had a series of jobs. They lack the common thread and the upward movement that would make their work experience a career.

There is, however, a work experience that is more than a job, more even than a career. It is what has traditionally been called a vocation. It is an inner drive to perform a particular kind of work. It is what Scripture calls one's *gift* (1 Peter 4:10).

A Vocation

A recent article in a national publication profiled Tom Moser of New Gloucester, Maine.[3] A former college professor, Moser had left teaching to become owner-operator of Thomas Moser Cabinet Makers, a $530,000-a-year company producing fine handcrafted furniture. The year before Moser made his decision to go into business for himself, he had been getting up at 5:30 every morning to go to his back porch workshop, where he rebuilt derelict antiques. "I loved being a professor," Moser remarked ten years after making his career switch, "but it was not what got me up in the morning."

The story of Tom Moser illustrates the crucial difference between a *job* and a *vocation*. A job is simply what we get paid to do. A vocation, however, is what gets us up in the morning.

Tom Moser may be unusual in being able to express his vocation by means of paid employment, but he is not unusual in *having* a vocation.

While researching this book, I conducted in-depth interviews with a variety of individuals engaged in different occupations. One was a noted oceanographic research scientist who still was working in his laboratory at the age of eighty. Another was the first female radio personality in a major Southwestern city. I talked to one man who had left a successful career in the booming California computer industry to enter the Christian ministry. During the course of these and many other similar conversations, I made an interesting discovery. All of these people were expressing to me the same *kinds* of feelings and experiences relating to their work—this despite the fact that the range of their work was so varied. The common element in all of their experiences seemed to be that all were doing what they felt called to do. Their work grew out of a deep, inner motivation. I realized that what I was seeing was the expression of what, in Christian teaching, had traditionally been called a vocation. During the course of my interviews and of my ongoing research into the psychology of career choice, I came to believe that everyone has at least the germ of a vocation. Furthermore, I became convinced that the most happy and satisfied workers are those whose job is part of a career as well as a vocation.

Our society, however, has difficulty accepting the idea that an individual might be called to a particular vocation. For one thing, our society encourages us to keep our work separate from our religious beliefs. Consequently, we find it difficult to relate what we do from nine to five to any sense of inner calling. We have difficulty with the word vocation believing that it properly refers only to religious calling or that, if it is understood to have a wider meaning, it refers only to the experience of very unusual and highly gifted people.

In fact, evidence of the universality of vocation comes from the work of pioneering psychologist Charlotte Bühler. Starting in the 1930s, Bühler did research into the identification of adult life cycles, focusing on the discovery of unifying themes that were to be found throughout the life of the individual. One of her discoveries was that, toward the end of a person's life, he often sums up the relative success of his life in terms of what he believes he should have achieved. Toward the end of a person's life, Bühler observed, an individual often seems to perceive very clearly the work he was suited for, the work he or she should have pursued.[4] Bühler's observation suggests that each person does in fact have a vocation, whether or not he expressed it effectively during the course of his life.

Vocation, in the sense of a deep-seated, inner drive to express a particular work, seems to have several characteristics. Understanding these characteristics is helpful in relating the concept of vocation to our own lives and in discovering the vocation to which God is calling us.

First, it is my belief, on the basis of Scripture, the evidence of modern psychology, and my own observations, that vocation is a universal gift. By that I mean that every person has at least the germ of a vocation. Scripture tells us that *"Each has received a gift"* (1 Peter 4:10). Notice the word *each*. Not just *some* people. Not just a handful of specially gifted people. *Each* has received a gift. In chapter two of this book I give examples of individuals who are living out a gift of vocation in a variety of different fields, and I show how you can begin to recognize characteristics of vocation in your own life.

Second, I believe that the nature of what we are called to do, as individuals, is consistent with the nature of our individual personalities. In chapter three I show how to understand the nature of *your* individual personality and how to relate this knowledge to the requirements of a job or career you may be considering.

Third, I believe that God gives each one of us a sense of inner direction in order to recognize the nature of the call he is leading us to, as well as the gifts and abilities to *express* our call. In chapter four, I show how to recognize the nature of God's call to you, as it has been revealed through your hopes and dreams, and how to discover the gifts and abilities God has given you.

Finally, I believe that God means for each of us not only to discover our true vocation, but to express it effectively in the world. Scripture says, in the passage we have cited previously, "As each has received a gift, *employ it for one another*." In chapters six through eleven, I help to explore the best place to use your gift, whether in your present job, in a new career, by means of self-employment, or through volunteering, and I discuss practical tools for obtaining employment consistent with your vocation. Such tools include personal goal-setting, writing a résumé, obtaining job recommendations, and developing effective interviewing skills.

This book was written in order that I might give you a road map for discovering *what* you want to do, and *how* to begin to express that, starting right where you are.

My hope is that you may discover for yourself a life work that is exciting and engaging, one that is more than simply "earning a living"—not just something that Mom or Dad or your teacher always thought you would be "good at," and not what life circumstances have programmed you into. Rather, it should be your own unique, distinctive, never to be exactly duplicated by anyone but you *thing*, something that is, in fact, your own *vocation*—that unique call that God has given you.

We will begin by observing people who have already found their vocation. We will look at these people in the next chapter and see what they can teach us about choosing the right work. As we do so, we may discover that you have already been expressing many aspects of your own vocation.

Chapter Two

You Don't Have to Be Miserable!

"I scream, sweat, jump, stomp. My feelings are totally engrossed. Painting is my passionate communication."
                                    —Mexican artist Leonardo Nierman

"The less I work, the less I enjoy it."
                                    —U. S. Senator William Proxmire

Wouldn't it be exciting if you could express in your daily life and work the very vocation God has given you? Wouldn't it be great if you could earn your living performing work for which you feel a strong inner motivation?

Believe it or not, there are people in a variety of fields who have succeeded in doing just that.

Such a person is Kitti Johnson, public affairs director of KYXY radio in San Diego, California, at the time I spoke to her, and one of the first women to break into broadcasting in San Diego.

When I interviewed Kitti for this book, she shared the fact that she had first sensed the road she was to take as early as third grade. Asked to write a composition on "What I Want to Be When I Grow Up," Kitti wrote that she wanted to be a radio and television producer—this at a time when such positions were closed to women.

After school, Kitti had several early jobs that did *not* relate to her first interest. One was being a manager of a shopping center. She remembers paging people over the intercom and thinking, "There must be more than this, although what I want to do is somehow connected to this." Kitti also worked as a travel agent and as a secretary. "Even as I was doing them they did not seem to be the thing I was supposed to be doing," Kitti remarked to me.

Today one of the successful and respected professionals in the broadcasting field, Kitti states that she likes all aspects of her radio work. Asked what she would do if, for some reason, she could not continue in radio broadcasting, she replies that she would do television—certainly a similar goal. "It's hard for me to imagine not doing this," Kitti admits.

Kitti Johnson is one of the fortunate people who has more than a job—more even than a career. She has a *vocation* for what she does. For Kitti and for others like her, their preferred style of relating to people, their abilities, the circumstances in which they like to work, and their inner motivation for achievement—all are consistent with the work they are paid to do.

In researching this book and conducting interviews with people in a variety of fields who, like Kitti, love their work, I discovered that, when we are doing what we like to do by living out the vocation that God has given us, we generally experience it in terms of six major characteristics. These characteristics seem to be present whether our vocation is to be a radio personality, an oceanographer, or a bank president. Read over the six characteristics described in this chapter. As you do so, ask yourself this question: What kinds of activities have, for you, these same characteristics?

—*Magnetic.* The activity pulls us to it. We experience a strong compulsion to do the things we know we enjoy doing.

—*Consistent.* The kinds of things we enjoy have not changed greatly over the course of our life. Even as a child we enjoyed doing the same general kinds of things.

—*Self-expressive.* What we really enjoy is so much a reflection of the person we are—our interests, values, our own unique abilities—that it is hard for us to imagine *not* doing them.

—*Pleasurable.* Doing what we enjoy is fun! It is more deeply satisfying and enjoyable than anything else we can imagine doing.

—*Energizing.* Doing what we enjoy *generates* energy

for us. The more of it we do, the more energy we have to do even more of this same kind of thing.

—*Perceived as valuable and important.* The things we really enjoy we tend to invest with a universal value. We come to believe that it is important for us (or at least for *somebody*) to be doing these particular kinds of activities in the world.

We will now look at these characteristics in more detail. As we do so, ask yourself again this question: *What are the things in my life that have—for me—these same characteristics?*

Your Vocation Is Magnetic

In the late nineteenth century, a farm boy was growing up on his father's farm in Michigan. This farm boy hated farming. What he loved was tinkering with machinery. Any broken machinery on the farm he would fix. When he ran out of things to fix on his father's farm, he looked for things to fix on his neighbors' farms. At sixteen, he followed his natural bent and left the farm to become a machinist for eight years. At twenty-four, possibly bowing to pressure from his father, he returned to the farm. Within two years he had confirmed again that the farm was not for him, and he was back in the city as a machinist. By this time he had a dream: He would build a motorcar. For the next seven years he worked nights in his garage, after work, to build an automobile that would be an improvement on the crude models that had been developed by others. In 1896 he believed he had succeeded in creating such an automobile. He helped organize an automobile company to manufacture the car. A year later he was out of a job. The company had failed. Undeterred, he helped found another motor company. This one, too, failed after only a year. In 1903 he made a third attempt. This one succeeded, and the Ford Motor Company went on to manufacture millions of cars. Henry Ford, the farm boy turned tinkerer, went on to change the face of American industry.[1]

The magnetic quality of Henry Ford's love of "tinkering," although dramatic, is not unique. Consider these examples:

—American playwright Tennessee Williams continues writing for twenty-two years before recognition comes at the age of thirty-four with his play *The Glass Menagerie.* Later in life, he remarks about people who want to write, "If they're meant to be writers, they will write. It may kill them."[2]

—Inventor Thomas Edison, employed as a telegrapher on the railroad, turns his boxcar into a laboratory and spends his time inventing electrical devices when he is supposed to be sending messages.[3]

—Abbie Hoffman, one of the protest leaders of the 1960s American counter-culture, a fugitive from justice for six years, risks his cover by organizing his community to battle industrial threats to the environment. Later, explaining why he got involved in an activity that threatened to blow his cover, he replied, "I've been an organizer for twenty years. . . . It's what I've been doing. It's what I'll go on doing."[4]

—A woman in San Diego starts her own successful direct mail business, spurred on by a former boss who tells her, "You ought to start your own business—you've been running everybody else's!"[5]

The fact is, all of these individuals had vocations for what they were doing. Their work drew them like a magnet. In the words of career experts Arthur Miller and Ralph Mattson,

> A person who is motivated to teach others will do so (or strive to do so), regardless of whether or not that is what is needed. A person motivated to innovate will so strive, even though it is not needed or wanted. Someone motivated to "put the house in order" will do so, even though everybody else can see eight other priorities needing more attention. Each of us perceives what needs to be done in a way which allows us to do what we are motivated to accomplish.[6]

Which activities in your life are "magnetic" for *you*? What kinds of involvements draw *you* like a magnet? What would *you* do for free, for the joy of doing it? Answer these questions, and you have begun to identify some of the *magnetic* elements of *your* vocation.

Your Vocation Is Consistent

The things you really enjoy doing are not things that you suddenly *start* doing at a certain time in your life. Generally these things are the same *kinds* of activities that you have enjoyed throughout your life.

Sculptor Henry Moore was known throughout the world for his huge, rounded sculptures of the human form. "When I was eight," Moore remembered, "my mother began to suffer rheumatism. As the youngest of the children, I was available for rubbing her back when the pain was most acute. . . . I learned from that the structure of the human back, and what three-dimensionality is all about."[7]

Many boys may have been asked to rub their mother's backs upon occasion. But how many carry a distinct memory of that experience? The point is, even at the age of eight, Henry Moore knew there was something important about that experience for him, something that would stay with him for the rest of his life.

Consider, for example:

—Hollywood director Steven Spielberg, known for the startling effects of many of his movies, remembers taking his inexpensive Kodak movie camera with him on family outings as a boy. On one occasion he convinced his mother to boil cherries jubilee in a pressure cooker until it exploded, so that he could film the messy crimson results on the kitchen walls and floor.[8]

—Humorist Erma Bombeck was writing a humor column as a twelve-year-old schoolgirl in Dayton, Ohio.

—Consumer activist Ralph Nader was organizing a campus campaign against spraying the trees with DDT as an undergraduate at Princeton University.[9]

—Pioneering heart surgeon Michael Debakey remembers learning sewing from his mother, as a boy, and also enjoying tinkering with the family car, two activities that, he once remarked, were similar to performing cardiovascular surgery.[10]

—Art collector Joseph Hirshorn, as a child, cut out pictures of famous art and tacked them up over his bed. In 1974 he donated his lifetime collection of four thousand paintings and two thousand sculptures to the Smithsonian Institute to form the basis of the Hirshorn Museum and Sculpture Garden.[11]

—Father Nicholas Reveles, a Roman Catholic priest as well as a musician and composer, whom I interviewed for this book, remembers distinctly his third Christmas, when he was given a toy piano. He remembers also occasions as a child when he could not sleep because musical compositions were playing in his head.

The list could go on. What is true of these notable personalities is true of each one of us. Like them, we too have tended to gravitate toward certain kinds of involvements. Our interests have in fact been more consistent than we realize, from childhood on.

What kinds of activities have *you* tended to gravitate toward? What has been the consistent pattern of *your* involvements? If you were asked to pick *one notable achievement* from each five-year period of your life, which kinds of achievements do you think you might mention? Answer these questions, and you will be beginning to identify some of the *consistent* elements of your own vocation.

Your Vocation Is Self-Expressive

The things you really enjoy doing are so exact a reflection of the *person* you are—your interests, your values, your abilities, your style of relating to people—that these activities become part of your self-identity as a person. It is hard to think of yourself, or for others to think of you, without thinking at the same time of these favorite things you like to do.

Comedian Mickey Rooney once referred to performing as his *"first* nature."[12] In a similar vein, writer Franz Kafka remarked, "I don't have 'literary *interests,'* literature is what I'm *made* of."[13]

The fascinating thing about the people I interviewed for this book, people who were in love with their work, was the fact that *they were unable to imagine themselves not doing what they do.* When I asked them what they would do if, for some reason, they were unable to continue to be employed as they were, they tended to answer in terms of some variation of what they were already doing. Radio personality Kitti Johnson, for example, remarked to me that, if she could not work in radio she would choose to work in television, and then said, "It's really the same thing, isn't it!"

The other fascinating thing about people who truly love their work is that typically they never completely "retire." How else to explain such people as Picasso, illustrator Norman Rockwell, anthropologist Margaret Mead, conductor Arthur Fiedler, comedian George Burns—who continued to work productively into their eighties and even nineties? Typical is Dr. Dennis Fox, professor emeritus at Scripps Institute of Oceanography in La Jolla, California, to whom I spoke just before his eightieth birthday.

"I love my work," Dr. Fox said to me in his office overlooking the Pacific, the scene of over half a century of scientific research in the field of marine biochemistry. "I *must* do research. I *must* experiment. I *must* write reviews. I'm in my eightieth year, but I'm still just as avid for learning as I ever was."

What kinds of activities are "self-expressive" of *you*? What kinds of things can you literally not imagine yourself *not* doing, and still be *you*? Answer these questions, and you have identified some of the *self-expressive* aspects of your vocation.

Your Vocation Is Pleasurable

Doing the things you really enjoy is more deeply pleasurable than anything else you can imagine doing with your time. "Enjoyment, in human life, isn't a fluke," writer Richard Bolles states in his best-selling guide to choosing a career, *What Color Is Your Parachute?* "It's part of God's plan. God wants us to eat; therefore God designs us so that eating is enjoyable. God wants us to sleep; therefore God designs us so that sleeping is enjoyable. . . . *God gives us unique (or at least unusual) skills and talents; therefore God designs us so that, when we use them, they are enjoyable.*"[14]

"If what you are doing you wouldn't pay to do, then that isn't God's highest will for you," remarks Elizabeth Kelly, founder of an Episcopal religious order on the West Coast.[15]

What kinds of activities are deeply personal for *you*? What would you *pay* to do? Which of your skills and abilities do you find deeply rewarding to use? Answer these questions and you are identifying some of the *pleasurable* aspects of your vocation.

Your Vocation Is Energizing

Doing what you enjoy generates mental, physical, and emotional energy. The more you do, the more you want to do. Lawrence Waddy, a man with a dual vocation of writer as well as Episcopal priest and himself a man who exudes a sense of physical and mental energy, remarks that people who express their vocation seem to have "a kind of springiness."[16]

Unlike activities for which you have little or no interest, that tend to drain your energy over a period of time, doing activities related to your vocation actually builds energy. Sometimes simply thinking about your favorite activity creates a rush of energy in anticipation of doing them.

What kinds of activities can *you* do for hours at a time without feeling drained or depleted? What things are you doing when you later remark, "I don't know where the time went"? What activities do you typically think about when you experience that anticipatory surge of energy? Answer these questions and you are identifying the *energizing* aspects of your vocation.

Your Vocation Is Perceived as Valuable and Important

The things that we really enjoy we tend to think of as valuable and important in and of themselves. The world is a better place, we believe, because we (or at least *somebody*) does these particular things.

James Hubbell is a San Diego artist whose exquisite work in tile, stained glass, and other media graces local churches, restaurants, and other public buildings. When I interviewed him he was busy laying tile for the floor of one of the buildings on his property in Julian, California. "When I put a piece of tile down here," Hubbell remarked, "that tile's not only right with the one next to it, but it's right with the tile up there, and it's right with the whole universe. One of the things we're trying to do is put the whole world back together." Hubbell's thoughts are similar to those expressed on one occasion by Hollywood director Steven Spielberg, "I never felt life was good enough, so I had to embellish it."[17] The point is, doing the things we *really* enjoy is seen as somehow *completing* the world. The world would be a poorer place, we believe, if we did not do it.

Which activities in your life have value and importance for *you*? What do *you* do that would leave the world a poorer place if you did not do it? Which activities in your life do you get really excited to tell others about? Answer this and you are identifying the nature of your vocation that *you* perceive to be valuable and important.

Your Vocation and Your Personality

In this chapter we have looked at what we can learn about the nature of fulfilling work by observing people who love their work. We have seen that, when people are doing work they enjoy, they experience their work as magnetic, consistent, self-expressive, pleasurable, energizing, valuable, and important. We have seen that we can use these characteristics as a guide for helping us discover what *we* like to do—what constitutes *our* vocation.

In the next section of the book, we will begin to explore in more detail exactly what it is *you* really like to do—the nature of *your* vocation. We will begin by exploring the relation between your vocation and your personality. God has given each one of us a personality that is unique. Together with your physical makeup, your personality is what makes you *you*. One of the key predictors of job satisfaction and success is how well the needs of your personality are met by the demands and challenges of the work you do. In the next chapter we will see how psychologist Carl Jung has provided a valuable key for understanding your personality in a way that is helpful in assisting you in making the right career choices.

Part Two

Five Steps to Career Satisfaction and Success

Chapter Three

Step One—Understand Your Personality

"Each has received a gift. . . ."   —1 Peter 4:10

I remember some years ago standing at an airline check-in counter at O'Hare International Airport in Chicago. Passengers were lined up ten deep at the counter. The ticket agent, a pleasant and efficient looking woman in her mid-thirties, was coping successfully with a barrage of passenger questions and concerns. "What time is the next flight to Denver?" "At what gate do I get American Airlines Flight 463 to Salt Lake City?" "Do you have a seat near a window in nonsmoking?" "Is the flight to Cincinnati still on time?" While answering these questions, she was constantly calling up information on the computer and relaying it to passengers. In addition to all of this, about every half minute the phone would ring, as somebody from outside would call in for flight information. Throughout all this confusion, she remained cool, confident, and pleasant, and gave every indication that she was thoroughly enjoying her job—a job that probably would have driven others to distraction!

What was her secret?

Her secret was that she probably was an extraverted sensation feeling type, and therefore had a gift for the work she was doing.

This terminology comes from the discoveries of psychologist Carl Jung, one of the founders of modern psychology. Jung developed a theory of personality that has gained wide acceptance and which has profound implications for an individual's choice of work.

The Bible says that each person has received a gift. The "gift" is a combination of two things. It is *what* we choose to do—that is, the nature of the work we perform. And it is *how* we do it—that is, the temperament, or personality characteristics, we bring to it. Our vocation, then, is to express the gift God has given us by means of our work in the world.

It is probably our temperament, more than any other single factor, that helps explain our preference for a certain kind of work. Carl Jung has given us a valuable tool for understanding our temperament, and therefore for understanding the nature of the vocation to which we are called. Jung believed that each individual demonstrates in his or her personality the interplay of four pairs of opposing characteristics. Understanding the nature of these characteristics, and how they relate to job satisfaction and success, can help us choose a work consistent with our temperament and in accordance with the vocation that God has given us.

Extraversion vs. Introversion

The first of Jung's opposing pairs is extraversion vs. introversion. These terms have come into common usage in our society. We tend to think of extraverts as the "life of the party" and introverts as shy and withdrawn. Actually, as Jung intended them, these terms have a different meaning. Extraverts are simply people who are primarily related to the *outer* world. Their attention and energies flow toward people, things, and situations "out there." Introverts, on the other hand, tend to focus on their own subjective reactions to the world.

Extraverts and introverts tend also to differ in their style of relating to people. Extraverts enjoy relating to many people, even if only on a superficial basis. Introverts, however, prefer to relate to a smaller number of people, often on a more intimate basis. An extravert will go to a party and, after two hours, is still raring to go. An introvert, on the other hand, has had enough and is more than ready to go home. Needless to say, this differing style of relating to people has important implications for the career choices of extraverts and introverts.

Generally speaking, extraverts will tend to be attracted to—

and do well at—jobs that bring them into daily contact with the "real world " of people, things, and situations. The busy executive running the affairs of a great company is an example of this outer-directed type. Introverts, however, will tend to seek jobs that will allow them to make creative use of their inner world of thoughts, impressions, and feelings. The artist in the studio or the psychologist in the counseling center are examples of this more inner-directed type. In addition, extraverts, more than introverts, will often tend to seek positions involving a greater degree of relating to people.

Intuition vs. Sensation

The second of Jung's opposing pairs is intuition vs. sensation. Intuitive types are able to make mental connections between one seemingly unrelated idea and another, and may experience flashes of insight that lead to new understandings at work or new and better ways of accomplishing a task. Intuition may give them the ability to read other people's facial expressions and body language. They may have a "sixth sense" about them. Successful salespeople may be intuitive types. Intuitives may also tend to seek out positions where they can relate ideas and concepts from a variety of disciplines. The ministry and teaching are examples of these.

Sensation types literally relate to the world on the basis of their senses. They live in a world of *things* and *facts*. Without a high degree of formal education, sensation types will tend to work with their hands. Skilled plumbers, carpenters, and electricians are often sensation types, as are also efficient secretaries. Highly educated sensation types will tend to seek out positions where they work with *facts*. Tax accountants and engineers are often sensation types.

Thinking vs. Feeling

The third of the opposing pairs is thinking vs. feeling. Thinking types approach the world logically and rationally. They tend to look at a situation and say, "Now let's just calm down and figure out what we should do about this." Thinking types tend to seek out positions where their critical, logical, rational faculty may be used to best advantage. Executives are often thinking types.

Feeling types relate to people and to situations on a feeling basis. They will confront the same situation as the thinking types and say, "Oh! This is terrible!" or "This is wonderful!" as the case may be. Feeling types empathize with others' joys and disappointments and are often "people persons." They tend to seek positions where they can relate to others on a one-to-one basis. An empathetic elementary school teacher, a nurse, a social worker, or a minister may be feeling types.

Judging vs. Perceiving

The last and final pair of opposites is judging vs. perceiving. Judging types tend to have firmly formed opinions about people and situations, and about what is right and wrong. They tend also to have a strong inner need to make decisions and to have matters settled. Consequently, they may seem to others strong and decisive. Judging types are drawn to occupations in which decisions have to be made and procedures have to be either articulated or followed. The crisply efficient business executive or office manager may be a judging type. A danger of judging types is the tendency to decide prematurely, before all the facts are in.

Perceiving types are more inclined to look at a situation and simply accept it for what it is, without the need to render a judgment on it. Consequently, they may appear more open-minded than judging types. Their openness to people and to situations may enable them to perceive them with more complexity—and sometimes with more accuracy. Without a strong inner need to make decisions and have matters settled, they may sometimes appear (and in fact may be) indecisive. Perceiving types do well in occupations in which it is important to see people and situations for what they are. The objective newspaper reporter gathering facts for a story may be a perceiving type.

How to Identify Your Type

Your type consists of your four highest characteristics drawn from each pair:

E extraversion	vs.	I introversion
N intuition	vs.	S sensation
T thinking	vs.	F feeling
J judging	vs.	P perceiving

Suppose, for example, that you are an introverted sensation feeling judging type. You would represent this by the letters ISFJ. In a similar manner you would represent the other fifteen possible letter combinations given by the four pairs. Each of these types has its particular strengths and weaknesses. Each type suggests different occupations for which that particular type is suited. Summaries of the sixteen different types are given on the chart on the next two pages.[1]

There are several ways to identify your type:

—Read over the type descriptions in this chapter. Decide which of each of the four pairs seems to describe you better. When you have decided, construct the four-letter combination that you believe most accurately describes your personality, and then refer to the chart on the following two pages.

—For a more accurate assessment, buy the book entitled *Please Understand Me*, by David Keirsey and Marilyn Bates, listed in the notes for this chapter.[2] Answer the questions in the self-scoring "Keirsey Temperament Sorter" contained in this book.

—If you plan to make a career decision based on a knowledge of your temperament according to the principles described in this chapter, I strongly advise going to your local college or university counseling center, or to a private counselor, and ask to be

Sensing Types

ISTJ Serious, quiet, earn success by concentration and thoroughness. Practical, orderly, matter-of-fact, logical, realistic and dependable. See to it that everything is well organized. Take responsibility. Make up their own minds as to what should be accomplished and work toward it steadily, regardless of protests or distractions.	**ISFJ** Quiet, friendly, responsible and conscientious. Work devotedly to meet their obligations. Lend stability to any project or group. Thorough, painstaking, accurate. May need time to master technical subjects, as their interests are usually not technical. Patient with detail and routine. Loyal, considerate, concerned with how other people feel.
ISTP Cool onlookers—quiet, reserved, observing and analyzing life with detached curiosity and unexpected flashes of original humor. Usually interested in impersonal principles, cause and effect, how and why mechanical things work. Exert themselves no more than they think necessary, because any waste of energy would be inefficient.	**ISFP** Retiring, quietly friendly, sensitive, kind, modest about their abilities. Shun disagreements, do not force their opinions or values on others. Usually do not care to lead but are often loyal followers. Often relaxed about getting things done, because they enjoy the present moment and do not want to spoil it by undue haste or exertion.
ESTP Matter-of-fact, do not worry or hurry, enjoy whatever comes along. Tend to like mechanical things and sports, with friends on the side. May be a bit blunt or insensitive. Adaptable, tolerant, generally conservative in values. Dislike long explanations. Are best with real things that can be worked, handled, taken apart and put together.	**ESFP** Outgoing, easygoing, accepting, friendly, enjoy everything and make things more fun for others by their enjoyment. Like sports and making things. Know what's going on and join in eagerly. Find remembering facts easier than mastering theories. Are best in situations that need sound common sense and practical ability with people as well as with things.
ESTJ Practical, realistic, matter-of-fact, with a natural head for business or mechanics. Not interested in subjects they see no use for, but can apply themselves when necessary. Like to organize and run activities. May make good administrators, especially if they remember to consider others' feelings and points of view.	**ESFJ** Warm-hearted, talkative, popular, conscientious, born cooperators, active committee members. Need harmony and may be good at creating it. Always doing something nice for someone. Work best with encouragement and praise. Little interest in abstract thinking or technical subjects. Main interest is in things that directly and visibly affect people's lives.

Introverts

Extraverts

Associated with Each Type

Intuitive Types

INFJ Succeed by perseverance, originality, and desire to do whatever is needed or wanted. Put their best efforts into their work. Quietly forceful, conscientious, concerned for others. Respected for their firm principles. Likely to be honored and followed for their clear convictions as to how best to serve the common good.	**INTJ** Usually have original minds and great drive for their own ideas and purposes. In fields that appeal to them, they have a fine power to organize a job and carry it through with or without help. Skeptical, critical, independent, determined, often stubborn. Must learn to yield less important points in order to win the most important.
INFP Full of enthusiasms and loyalties, but seldom talk of these until they know you well. Care about learning, ideas, language, and independent projects of their own. Tend to undertake too much, then somehow get it done. Friendly, but often too absorbed in what they are doing to be sociable. Little concerned with possessions or physical surroundings.	**INTP** Quiet, reserved, impersonal. Enjoy especially theoretical or scientific subjects. Logical to the point of hairsplitting. Usually interested mainly in ideas, with little liking for parties or small talk. Tend to have sharply defined interests. Need careers where some strong interest can be used and useful.
ENFP Warmly enthusiastic, high-spirited, ingenious, imaginative. Able to do almost anything that interests them. Quick with a solution for any difficulty and ready to help anyone with a problem. Often rely on their ability to improvise instead of preparing in advance. Can usually find compelling reasons for whatever they want.	**ENTP** Quick, ingenious, good at many things. Stimulating company, alert, and outspoken. May argue for fun on either side of a question. Resourceful in solving new and challenging problems, but may neglect routine assignments. Apt to turn to one new interest after another. Skillful in finding logical reasons for what they want.
ENFJ Responsive and responsible. Generally feel real concern for what others think or want, and try to handle things with due regard for other person's feelings. Can present a proposal or lead a group discussion with ease and tact. Sociable, popular, sympathetic. Responsive to praise and criticism.	**ENTJ** Hearty, frank, decisive, leaders in activities. Usually good in anything that requires reasoning and intelligent talk, such as public speaking. Are usually well-informed and enjoy adding to their fund of knowledge. May sometimes be more positive and confident than their experience in an area warrants.

Introverts

Extraverts

given the Myers-Briggs Types Indicator. The counselor will explain to you the significance of the results. In this way you will avoid possible errors of personal judgment in attempting to do your self-assessment. Finally, if you are interested in reading more about how type affects career choice, you may wish to purchase the book by David Keirsey and Marilyn Bates, mentioned above, or *Gifts Differing*, by Isabel Briggs Myers, listed in the chapter notes.[3]

Type and Occupation: Some Examples

How does personality type affect work choice and career satisfaction? Let's take a couple of examples.

Example One. You and your spouse are looking forward to going out to dinner at a fine restaurant. What type do you hope your waiter will be, in order for you two to have a pleasant evening out? Let's look at the pairs, one by one:

Extraversion vs. introversion (E vs. I). You would probably want an extraverted type. You want the person who serves you to greet you in a friendly manner and help you feel at home.

Intuition vs. sensation (N vs. S). You want a sensation type. You don't want someone who is so busy thinking about the problems of the world that he forgets who gets the split pea soup and never gets around to bringing the rolls.

Thinking vs. feeling (T vs. F). You want feeling. You want him to *care* whether you and your spouse are comfortable and having a good time.

Perception vs. judging (P vs. J). You want perception. You want him simply to "take in" the situation at your table. You are not interested in having him reflect on whether or not he approves of your taste in clothes this evening.

In conclusion, if you and your spouse went out to dinner, you might hope that your waiter would be an extraverted sensation feeling perception type—an ESFP. If he were, the chances are that the two of you would have a most enjoyable evening out.

Example Two. April 15 is just around the corner. You are getting ready to put your financial records in the hands of a tax accountant. What type would you hope your tax accountant would be, in order to increase the chances that she will prepare your returns carefully and accurately? Again, let's look at the pairs:

Extraversion vs. introversion (E vs. I). You probably want an introverted type. You want someone who enjoys sitting alone in a room working with figures. If she enjoys it, the chances are greater that she will be good at it.

Intuition vs. sensation (N vs. S). You want sensation. You want someone absolutely accurate with facts and figures. Intuition is of little use in this situation.

Thinking vs. feeling (T vs. F). You want thinking. You don't care how she *feels* about your tax returns. You just want her to have a knowledge of the relevant IRS tax laws and how to apply them.

Perception vs. judging (P vs. J). You want judging. You want someone who is comfortable with the need to make a decision between two alternatives, someone who can say, *"This* is the way we will do it in this particular case."

The person who would most likely do a good job preparing your taxes, then, would be an introverted sensation thinking judging type—an ISTJ.

Does this mean that a member of a particular profession must be a particular "type"? Of course not! In reality there is a considerable range of types within any one profession. It simply means that personality type is *one* of the factors contributing to success in one's profession. It also means that knowing what your type is is helpful in enabling you to choose a career wisely—and for predicting your success and happiness in that career.

Now I Want to Ask Myself

When considering whether a particular job or career "fits" your personality type, and therefore may be the vocation to which God is calling you, consider carefully any strong requirements of your personality type and how they relate to any strong demands of the job or career you may be considering.

If, for example, you are considering a job where you must work with facts and figures all day—and be absolutely accurate—you really should be fairly high in sensation. If, instead, you are high in intuition (the opposite of sensation), you would be well advised to avoid a job of this nature. If you are high in introversion, you should probably avoid a job involving continuous contact with large numbers of people. In other words, you want to *avoid* a job that demands the *opposite* of the quality you possess. Here are some questions to ask yourself about any job or career:

Are you:	*Then you want to avoid jobs where:*
high in extraversion (low in introversion)	you are working alone most of the time, without a person-to-person contact.
high in introversion (low in extraversion)	you are continuously relating to large numbers of people.
high in intuition (low in sensation)	you are constantly dealing with facts and figures, and you must be absolutely accurate.
high in sensation (low in intuition)	you must demonstrate a lot of originality and creativity, and there are few agreed-upon procedures to follow.
high in thinking (low in feeling)	you must deal with people in a helping capacity, and continuously demonstrate a great deal of empathy for them.
high in feeling (low in thinking)	you spend most of your time working alone, at a desk or with tools or machines, with a minimal amount of time spent in one-on-one personal contact with people.
high in judging (low in perception)	you work in a situation in which there are few agreed-upon rules or procedures to follow.
high in perception (low in judging)	there is a constant need to make firm decisions, and to stick with them.

If you are currently employed, and if you look at the demands of your present job in relation to the needs of your personality type, you may become aware that the two do not complement each other. The first question you may ask is, "Will I *change*? If I just stay in my present job long enough, will my personality eventually *become* like that which the job requires?" The answer is, unfortunately, no—not to any significant degree. To be sure, there will be changes in your personal values and preferences over a period of time, and the nature of the work you do certainly influences these changes. An introvert working in an extraverted profession (sales or ministry, for example) will probably, over a period of time, learn to show a greater degree of extraversion. A perception type working in a situation where decisions constantly need to be made will, over a period of time, show an increase in judging capacity. But keep this in mind: Your basic personality type is formed at an early age. The tendency toward extraversion or introversion can be seen in a child as young as eighteen months.[4] By the time you are an adult, therefore, your basic personality type has been formed and will not alter to any significant degree. The trick is not to try to *change* your personality to fit your job or career. The trick is rather to change your job or career—if necessary—in order to fit your personalty type, and to live out the vocation to which God is calling you.

In this chapter we have looked at different personality types as described by psychologist Carl Jung. We have also seen how personality type affects one's choice of work and also tends to predict one's level of satisfaction *in* that work. But as you know, God has created you as more than a "type." God has created you as a unique individual, whose needs, abilities, interests, and dreams are totally unlike those of anyone else. In the next chapter we will explore the unique person you are and discover how knowing the *nature* of your uniqueness can assist you in making wise career choices, and in accordance with the vocation to which God is calling you.

Chapter Four

Step Two—Have Some Crazy Dreams

"Trust your own meaning, follow your own meaning, let it guide you."   —psychologist Carl Jung

"What are you seeking?"
                    —the mysterious stranger to Joseph in Genesis 37:15

You have had the conversation often before. A friend asks you what your plans are for the future. You mention several possible courses of action that seem to "make sense." Then your eyes light up as you think of some wild, crazy idea of something you've always wanted to do, and you find yourself saying, "What I *really* want to do. . . ."

One of the most difficult aspects about finding the work to which God is really calling you is the fact that you and I are so conditioned by all the well-meaning voices talking *at* us, telling us what we "should" do, that we often tend to lose touch with a sense of what it is *we* want to do—what God is calling us to do. This is not only a problem of our own day. Throughout the Bible we read of individuals withdrawing into the desert to rediscover a sense of direction for their lives. In the Old Testament the prophet Elijah searches in vain to hear the voice of God in the earthquake, wind, and fire—the tumult of daily living, if you will—but finally hears it in the "still, small voice."[1] In a similar fashion Paul retreated into the desert after his experience on the road to Damascus,[2] and we remember how Jesus often withdrew to the hills to pray. It seems that, in order to regain a sense of clarity, we need periodically to step back from the clamor of our daily lives.

The exercises that follow in this chapter are based on two assumptions. The first is that we already know what we want to do—the vocation to which God is calling us—deep down inside. What we need to do is simply reach that level of awareness, and apply the insights we gain to our own situation. This process is what career development expert Richard Nelson Bolles calls "fooling the left brain"—bypassing the logical, rational, "common sense" part of our mind in favor of a more unitive, right brain awareness. The second assumption is that what *we* want to do and what *God* wants us to do are often one and the same. In fact, it is often by means of our awareness of a strong drive to express ourselves in a particular way that we come to discover the nature of our own vocation.

In this chapter we are going to take what you *"really* want to do" and look at it seriously. What follows is a series of written exercises.[3] Read them over and decide which you would like to do. You don't have to do them all. Just do enough so that you feel a pattern of your hopes and dreams is beginning to emerge. Then turn to the section of this chapter entitled, "Now I Want to Ask Myself. . ." to find out how to interpret what you have written.

A word of advice about how to do these exercises. Try as much as possible to get away from distractions in your environment while you are doing them. Find yourself a quiet place and time. Better still, get away completely—to the beach or mountains—and give yourself "space" where your mind and thoughts can run free.

Finally, if you absolutely *hate* writing and simply cannot stand the idea of sitting down with paper and pencil, do these exercises by talking into a tape recorder. You can do this by yourself or, if you prefer, you can direct your remarks to someone else. Then, afterwards, have someone type up what you said. That way, you will have a written record of your hopes and dreams. Finally, if nothing I have said so far appeals to you, and you are visually oriented, you might try illustrating some of these exercises. The point is, there are many ways of getting in touch with your heart's desires. The important thing is to begin.

1. Things That Really Bug Me About My Job

Take a sheet of paper. List everything you can think of that bugs you about your present job. Mention salary, working conditions, the nature of the work itself, your co-workers, or anything else. Be specific. Say exactly what it is that bugs you about each thing you have mentioned. Stop only when you feel you have come to the end of the things that really bother you about your present job.

2. The Detective in My House

There is a detective in your house, investigating the person who lives there (you). He is going from room to room, looking for clues as to your personality. Follow him as he goes around your house. Write down what he sees as he goes from room to room— the kind of books you read, pictures on your walls, hobbies you pursue, the kind of clothes in your closet. Then write down some conclusions he might draw about this person who lives in your house.

3. Letter to a Friend

It is five years from now. During the past five years, everything you have always wanted to achieve has come true. You are doing exactly what you want to do and living exactly the lifestyle you have always wanted to live. You are now writing to a friend in Europe, describing a typical day in your life. Be as specific as you can. Describe what your place of work looks like, your home, who you eat lunch with, the clothes you wear to work, what you earn— anything and everything you consider important or interesting. In order to do this exercise, imagine that you have solved whatever "practical problems" stand between you and achieving whatever it is you have always wanted to achieve.

4. My Fantastic Life

This exercise is a variation on the one above. In this exercise, instead of being the future, it is the present. You have *already* achieved everything you always wanted to achieve. You are doing it *now*! You are now looking back over your life up to this point and seeing how, at every step along the way, you made all the right decisions and all the right moves to lead you to where you are right now—which is where you always wanted to be. Write an autobiography of your life from childhood or from high school on, *as you would have wanted it to be.* Have fun. Pull out all the stops. Reinvent your life in accordance with your wildest dreams!

5. Heroes, Mentors, and Role Models

All of us can remember people whom we have admired. These may be people we have actually known. Or they may be people we have read about, or even characters in fiction or characters in the Bible. Write down the names of three or four people you have always admired. Now, in a short paragraph, write down everything you have known about each of these people. Write down exactly what it is you admire—and what qualities you identify with—in the lives of these individuals.

6. My Greatest Achievements

Think of three or four things that you have accomplished in your life that (1) you felt good about, and that (2) others gave you recognition for. Once you have thought of three or four such achievements, take a piece of paper and divide it into three columns, as shown below. Under "Success Story," simply write down in your own words exactly what it was you did. Write a short paragraph. Describe the event as you would to a four-year-old child. Under "Skills Used," write down single words that describe actions you needed to perform, or qualities you needed to possess, in order to accomplish what you did. Use "action verbs"—verbs ending in *ing*—like planning, coordinating, convincing, repairing, and so

forth. Jot down some personal characteristics, too, like persever-
ance or determination or creativity or mechanical ability, that
enabled you to accomplish whatever it was you accomplished. In
the last column, under "Why It Mattered," write in your own words
the importance of what you did, both for yourself and even for the
whole world! (A hint to get started: If you have problems thinking
of achievements, divide your life into five-year segments, such as
from age ten to fifteen, fifteen to twenty, and so forth, and then ask
yourself, if you had to pick *one* achievement from each of these five-
year periods, what would it be?)

Success Story	Skills Used	Why It Mattered

7. Childhood Memories

Often our games and activities reflect pretty accurately the
person we really are, before society starts shaping us to its own
demands. Write down the games and activities you remember
enjoying in childhood. If there were special activities that you
enjoyed alone, or if there were particular games that you remember
leading other children in, pay particular attention to these. What
was the first children's book that you remember making an impres-
sion on you as a child? What was it you liked about this book? Use
this exercise to get in touch with the person you were when you
were a child.

8. Go on a Pilgrimage

Throughout the centuries Christians have gone on pilgrimages in order to re-experience the sense of meaning embodied in particular sacred spots. In this exercise I would like you to imagine going on a pilgrimage to some "sacred spot" from your own personal past. Imagine some place and time that you have happy memories of—that you perhaps continue to think about from time to time even today. Go back to that place in your own mind. Where are you? What are you seeing? What is the first place you go to, in that particular spot? Let your thoughts and feelings flow freely as you enjoy a pilgrimage into an important part of your own past.

9. My "Peak Experience"

Psychologist Abraham Maslow called them "peak experiences"[4]—incidents of positive, heightened emotion, in which you feel on top of the world. All of us have had such experiences from time to time. Remember some peak experience you have had. Remember especially the one you may have had that occurred as a result of your accomplishing a particular thing—or *thinking* about accomplishing a particular thing. What do you remember about those incidents? What were the circumstances in which they took place? Above all, what was it that you accomplished, or dreamed about accomplishing, that seemed to trigger your peak experience?

10. Commissions

Throughout the Bible and down through Christian history, men and women have been commissioned to perform particular tasks for the good of the community. God's command to Moses to lead the people out of their bondage in Egypt is an example of such a commission.[5] In a less formal sense you and I are constantly being "commissioned" by our family friends, and neighbors when they ask us to do things based upon the gifts and abilities they recognize in us.

Try to remember any times people have asked you to take on a particular task for your church or a club or volunteer group. Write down what you remember about such incidents. What kinds of things have people asked you to do? Also, what is it that people have complimented you for over the years? Write down all the "strokes" you remember receiving in your life, and the reasons why you received them.

11. Green with Envy

Envy is usually considered a negative emotion. But envy can serve as a clue to the kinds of things that are really important to us. When we are "green with envy," we are usually in the presence of something that speaks to our own hopes and dreams. Think back to the occasions when you were "green with envy." Exactly what was it you were envious *about*? Write down, in as much detail as you can, what the circumstances were that caused you to feel such envy on these occasions.

12. Dreams: The "Royal Road" to the Unconscious

Throughout history dreams have been looked to as a source of inner guidance. In the Bible the Old Testament prophet Daniel gives King Nebuchadnezzar a reason for interpreting his dreams: "that you may know the thoughts of your mind."[6] In a similar fashion our own personal dreams often reveal to us the "thoughts of our mind" that are below the level of conscious awareness. For this reason Freud called dreams the "royal road" to the unconscious. Dreams can help show us why we may be frustrated with our present job and can help to suggest the nature of the work we are suited for —the vocation to which God is calling us.

If you remember a dream, especially one that seems to relate to your work, write down everything you remember about it. Write down the "plot line," the cast of characters, where the dream took place, and the emotions you experienced during various parts of the dream. After you have described the dream, add a section entitled, "Day's Events and Associations." Under this, jot down anything important or noteworthy that happened the day *before* you had the dream, and note the *date* of the dream. Then turn to the next part of this chapter to learn how to interpret this material.

Now I Want to Ask Myself. . .

You have done four or five of the exercises above. If you are very industrious, possibly you have done them all. Go back and reread what you have written. Underline any words or phrases that seem especially important. If you feel like it, make comments in the margin about what you have written. For example, rereading one of her exercises, one woman underlined the phrase "*helping people*" and then wrote in the margin, "It seems this has always been important to me." When you have reread your exercises and underlined words and phrases, turn to the section below, and answer the questions listed for the particular exercises you did.

1. Things That Really Bug Me About My Job

The first thing to ask yourself is this: "These things that I have listed that bug me about my present job—are they *situational*, or are they in the nature of the work itself?" A situational problem is one that pertains to the particular *place* where you work but not to the work itself. Change your place of work, and you have eliminated the problem. Problems in the nature of the work itself, however, are a different matter. If you are in sales and you hate working with people, then clearly you do not have a vocation for sales and you need more than a job change. You need to look at changing your whole *career*. So are the problems you listed situational, or are they basic to the nature of the work itself?

Now take the exercise one step further. Draw a second column where you listed the things that bug you. In this second column, write the *opposite* of the things you listed in column one. For example, if you listed "low pay" in column one, write "higher pay" in column two. If you wrote "lack of freedom on the job" in column one, write "more freedom on the job" in column two. When you have finished writing all the opposites for your list in column one, take a separate sheet of paper and list in order of importance for you the top five positive characteristics from column two. When you have completed this, you will have written a job description for the job you would like to have!

2. The Detective in My House

This exercise is based on the fact that the nature of our vocation is often suggested by the kind of living space we create for ourselves. At work our environment is chosen *for* us. At home we are free to express our interests and preferences by the pictures we hang, the clothes we wear, and the books we read.

Ask yourself first, what is the "heart" of my home? Every person thinks of one area of the home as the heart for them, the place where they can go and completely be themselves, either alone or with others. For one it may be the kitchen; for another, the workbench; for still another, the desk in the study. What is it for *you*? What does the heart of *your* home seem to suggest about your primary interests away from the job?

Now go to your bedroom. Look at the clothes in your closet. Which are your favorite ones? What do they suggest about your interests and values away from work?

Go to your living room or family room. Look at the books and magazines on your coffee table. What are they about? If you have your books arranged by subject area, which area seems to be growing?

Look at the pictures on your walls. Are they landscapes? Portraits or Animals? Houses? What do these pictures suggest about the nature of your *temperament*? Are they the kind of pictures a "people person" would be likely to have? Or do they suggest a preference for solitude?

When the detective in your house has completed his search, ask yourself what he has discovered about your interests, values, and preferences that could translate into the requirements for a job for which you might be suited.

Take, for example, one person who identified the kitchen as the heart of her home because family members and friends gathered there for a good time. "Surely you can't earn your living entertaining people in your kitchen," you say. Probably not. But you can ask what this preference means in *general* terms— and then translate this into the requirements for an existing job. A person for whom the heart of the home is the kitchen is one who enjoys being with and relating to people. No sitting in the back room typing for *this* person! The person whose workbench is the heart of the home is expressing different interests and personality needs. So also the person whose desk is the heart. As you read over the results of this exercise, do not expect to find absolute consistency in your interests. After all, we have *many* interests. But look for the central theme. Look to see which interests seem to reappear in various areas of your home. And then ask yourself how you might express these interests on a job in the "real world."

3. Letter to a Friend

Ask yourself first: What is the *major* focus of my activity in this fantasy? Am I primarily helping people? Expressing some kind of artistic creativity? Building or inventing something? What is the major thrust?

Now ask: What seems to be my preferred *style* of doing this activity? Do I see myself as being highly involved with other people? If so, in what capacity? Directing them? Teaching them? Selling to them? What? Or do I see myself working primarily alone? Also, what seems to be the nature of my *motivation*? Is it to make a lot of money? Or am I assuming in my fantasy that the money will simply *be* there, and that I am free to do this activity for its own sake?

Now compare your fantasy with the nature of your present employment. Do you see a *major* difference between your fantasy and how you earn your living? For example, does your fantasy show you highly involved with people on a one-to-one basis, while at work you sit in the back room with the firm's payroll records? If this is the case, you want to consider how you are going to integrate the interests and values you expressed in your fantasy into your present life.

After people complete this exercise, they sometimes ask: Just how literally should I take my fantasy? In other words, if you saw yourself living in a house in the country five years from now, is the house in the country something you really want? Or is it a *symbol* for something you really want? The answer is, probably both. Ask yourself: What does this house in the country *mean* to me? My guess is that it would represent a desire for privacy, a sense of personal "space," and the opportunity periodically to withdraw and recharge your batteries. Once you see it in this light, you begin to realize that *you can give yourself these same qualities right now*. Then, in five years, if you actually do acquire a house in the country, you have already been enjoying the very qualities that this house represents.

This "Letter to a Friend" exercise is one of my own personal favorites for getting in touch with my deepest desires and the things I really do want to achieve in my life. After you do this exercise, I suggest that you date it and then file the material away for safekeeping. Then, whenever you feel the urge, do this same exercise again. Look to see which of your expressed desires change or alter themselves. Look especially to see which of your expressed desires remain the same. These are likely to be the things that you really do want to achieve. Then, start working on achieving these things in your present life right now, building a solid base for the future that you want to have.

4. My Fantastic Life.

In interpreting this exercise, try to avoid a sense of regret or "could have beens" and concentrate instead on seeing the pattern of interests and values that have always been important to you. Read the questions for exercise three, "Letter to a Friend," above, and ask yourself similar questions for this exercise. What is the major focus of your activities in this fantasy? What seems to be your preferred style of operating? What seems to be the nature of your motivation? Now address yourself to your present life: How could you start *right now* doing some of the things you saw yourself doing during your "fantastic life"?

5. Heroes, Mentors, and Role Models

Of the three or four people you admire, what are some of the things they have in common? Is it how they earn their living? Is it some personal quality—for example, a strong sense of independence? Is it some aspect of their lifestyle? Do all live in the country, for example, or all have big families? Write down as many qualities as you can think of that they all share. Now look at your present life. Ask yourself: What is it that these people are expressing in their lives that I would like to express? How could I begin *right now* demonstrating some of these same qualities that I admire in these other people?

6. My Greatest Achievements

Pride in accomplishment is subjective. What one person is proud of, another finds boring. The point is, you can look to the nature of the things *you* are proud of in the past as an indicator of the kinds of things you enjoy—and that may suggest the nature of the vocation to which God is calling you.

Look first to the nature of the achievement you cited in column one. How would you describe it in general terms? Did it involve constructing something with your hands? Expressing artistic creativity? Working directly with people in order to teach them, direct them in a particular activity, or assist them to grow? How could you describe the general nature of this activity?

Now look at the second column. The action verbs and personal qualities that you listed are probably a very partial list of the many skills and personal strengths you drew upon in order to achieve the accomplishment in column one. What you listed in this column is a helpful reminder of the many skills and personal strengths that each of us possesses—and that we use every day of our lives.

Now look at your third column. What you were really describing here was the nature of your motivation for doing things you enjoy the most. Each of us is motivated by different rewards, and psychologists tell us that each of us is fairly consistent in the kind of rewards we look for. One characteristic of having found our vocation is that it provides for us exactly the *kind* of motivation that we need in order to feel fulfilled in our work. What kind of rewards are *you* looking for? Are you primarily motivated by the desire to help people? By the desire to make money? By the desire to prove yourself against impossible odds? What is the nature of *your* "turn on"? Now think about your present job. Is your present job providing you the kind of rewards that you experienced with your "greatest achievements"? If not, you need to question whether this is ultimately the work for you.

7. Childhood Memories

What do you remember about the special games you played as a child, especially the ones you played alone or that you "invented"? Often these games contain some real clues as to the nature of our deepest interests. One person of my acquaintance remembers coming home from school and lining up the sofa pillows on his bed and spending whole afternoons "teaching" them. Unsurprisingly, this person went on to become a teacher. What fantasies do *you* remember playing out as a child about what you wanted to be? Naturally, many of these childhood fantasies were unrealistic. But imbedded in the fantasies are often some important clues as to your real interests, values, and personal needs—qualities that remain with you even to this day. How did you relate to your friends as a child? Were you the "leader of the pack"? Were you the loyal follower? Were you the loner who preferred to spend time with one or two close friends, or by yourself? Very likely your childhood style of relating to people remains the same, to some degree, to this day. The children's book that you remember—what was it that appealed to you about the story? How might that relate to your life in the present? What do *you* remember about your childhood, and how do your childhood memories explain the person you are today?

8. Go on a Pilgrimage

Look at the places you have gone to and the people you have

seen in your imaginary pilgrimage. Why do you think you have chosen to go to these *particular* places and see these *particular* people? What patterns seem to be operating in your choice of people and places? One person doing this exercise discovered that the college campus on which he had grown up as a child and where, later, he had earned a Masters degree, represented the "heart" of his imaginary pilgrimage. From this experience he learned that the *values* represented by the college campus—learning, knowledge, the opportunity to teach others—were an integral part of his vocation and needed to be more fully integrated into the work he was doing.

9. My "Peak Experience"

Peak experiences are important because they often contain clues to the nature of our deepest motivations. Often they point the way to things that we actually accomplish later in life. A friend of mine, a minister in a local church, remembers a peak experience during his last year in seminary. He was walking the streets of the town on a beautiful spring evening just before graduation when he became tremendously excited about the possibility of teaching personal growth and self-discovery courses in the church. Ten years later, he is known in the church for the self-discovery courses he teaches. The point is, peak experiences are so deeply exciting and motivating precisely because, at such moments, we are so very much in touch with our real desires—desires which, if acted upon, often bring our greatest rewards.

What kinds of personal hopes and dreams seem suggested by your peak experience? Was it to be the founder of a great business? To make a world-changing scientific discovery? To change the nature of education? To create the ultimate in hand-crafted furniture? What was it that so *excited* you during your peak experience? And how could you begin to make that dream come true in your life right now?

10. Commissions

Read over the incidents you describe where people asked you

to do something or praised you for some personal quality or skill. Ask yourself: Is there a consistency in the kinds of *accomplishments* people have praised me for? Is there a consistency in the kinds of personal *qualities* people have praised me for? And how could I earn a living doing these same kinds of accomplishments and demonstrating these same kinds of personal qualities? Take, for example, one of the members of my first church. Let's call her Betty. People have often remarked on Betty's ability to take a group of volunteers, motivate them, organize them, and unite them around the completion of a common goal. Betty might ask herself: Where could I be paid for exercising my skills for group motivation and leadership? When Betty can answer this question to her own satisfaction, she has probably found the nature of her real work.

Besides identifying the consistent patterns in the nature of the accomplishments people have praised you for, ask yourself three additional questions. First, has more than one person praised you for a similar type of accomplishment? You need to "reality check" the reaction of one person against that of others to make sure the quality of your accomplishments in this area really stands up. Second, did the people who praised you for your accomplishments have an "axe to grind"? The father who tries to push his daughter into nursing when her real desire is to be an attorney is not *commissioning* her; he is *coercing* her! Third, are you personally *interested* in doing more of the kinds of activities for which you have been praised? You may have the *ability* to do something but not the slightest *interest* in doing it. Therefore, is this activity one in which both your interest and your abilities coincide?

11. Green with Envy

Read over your accounts of the times you felt a strong envy of what someone else accomplished. Are there common elements running through many of the incidents? For example, have you experienced envy on more than one occasion when you heard of some woman who had started her own business? Or how about the artist who lives on his farm in Maine? Or that successful executive running the affairs of a great corporation? The point is, different *kinds* of people and different *kinds* of achievements trigger envy in different individuals, depending upon their own unrealized dreams and ambitions. What can you learn from your own "green with envy" experiences? What parts of your own self are crying out for expression?

In interpreting the results of this exercise, it is important to ask yourself exactly what the element was in that other person's experience that made you so envious. Take the artist working out of his farm in Maine, for example. Were you envious of his opportunity to express personal creativity? Of his freedom as a self-employed person? Of the fact that he lived in the country? What was it that you identified with in his experience? And how could you move from being "green with envy" toward accomplishing these same kinds of things in your own life?

12. Dreams: The "Royal Road" to the Unconscious

Working with dreams to get a sense of inner guidance about what you should be doing with your life has one strong advantage—and also one strong disadvantage. The advantage is that dreams are probably the most accessible and safest way for the average person to get in touch with the riches of the unconscious. The disadvantage is that the language of dreams is symbolic, and therefore often difficult to understand. Furthermore, dreams do not confine themselves to addressing an area we may be concerned about, such as work, for example. We may look to our dreams for guidance about work and discover instead that they seem to be giving us advice about marriage! Because of the complexity of working with one's own dreams, you may wish to engage the services of a competent therapist.

In working with my own dreams over the years, I have found them to be invaluable aids in revealing to me, first, the nature of my frustrations and, second the nature of my "growing edge." By "growing edge" I mean simply those areas of my life that generate excitement in me and that point to new directions for the future.

Once you have written down several dreams, especially those that seem to relate in some way to work in general or to a sense of life direction, ask yourself two questions. First, what do your dreams suggest about how you feel about your current employment? Look for symbolic language and situations. Suppose you had a dream in which your work place turned into a house in which you found yourself trapped. Do you possibly feel "trapped" in your present job? The second question to ask yourself is, what seems to be your "growing edge"? What parts of your dream do you feel especially good about? What were you doing in the dream during those parts? How could the values or interests represented by this "growing edge" be more fully integrated into your work and your life?

For those who would like to know more about how to work with dreams, I have listed several useful books in the chapter notes.[7]

I've Done the Exercises. Now What Should I Do?

By now you have done several of the exercises and you have answered some of the questions suggested in this chapter. In working with the results, you have gained what may be some new insights about yourself—about the needs of your personality, your interests and values. At this point you may wish to talk over these insights with a good friend or perhaps your priest or minister. Get the reaction of this person to what you have written and what you believe you have discovered about yourself. He or she may help you to see additional patterns and connections that you were not aware of. Write down their reactions to the material you present to them, and file it away with the rest of the material from this chapter.

Doing several of these exercises should have helped get you in touch with some of your deepest values, interests, and personal needs—aspects of yourself that need to be expressed in the work you do, the vocation to which God is calling you. What you need to do now is to translate this new knowledge of yourself into the requirements for a job or career consistent with these values, interests, and needs. In the next chapter I will show you how to do that.

Chapter Five

Step Three—
Focus on a Goal

You have written out some of the exercises in the last chapter. What is your next step?

Your next step is to state in your own words the vocation to which God seems to be calling you. In doing this you will be identifying the name of a *real job*—one that someone will pay you to do—that is consistent with the needs of your personality, your interests and values, as they were revealed in the exercises in the last chapter.

In order to describe your vocation and thus identify your "ideal job," read over again your exercises. Pay special attention to the words and phrases that you underlined. Read again your margin comments. Notice especially the desires that you repeated in more than one exercise. These desires may refer to:

—*your preferred style of working with others*—your preference to work alone or, the opposite, your desire to be part of a team.
—*the nature of what you like to do*—to work in a creative situation, for example, or to work with facts and figures.
—*the setting in which you want to work*—outdoors in nature, for example, or in the middle of a bustling city.

Your desire may involve any of these factors or others as well. When you have finished rereading your exercises, take a separate sheet of paper and list all the desires you mentioned. When you are done, you should list a dozen or fifteen or twenty separate elements that you would like to have on your "ideal job."

Now take a pair of scissors and cut this sheet up, separating each item you listed. When you are done you will have a dozen or fifteen or twenty separate slips of paper, each listing an item of importance for you. Now arrange these slips in their order of importance for you. If the most important thing for you would be the *setting* in which you work, then this would come first. If the second most important thing would be your opportunity to express artistic creativity, then this will come second, and so forth. When you are done, you will have a list of job-related elements, arranged in order of importance for you. You are now ready to:

Write Your Own Goal Statement

A goal statement is simply putting into your own words what you would like to do and what you believe God is calling you to do. In employment-related terms, it is describing *a career direction that would seem to make sense for the person that you seem to be.* Look back to your list of job related elements. Then write down such a goal statement for yourself. My own personal goal statement, for example, reads like this:

—teaching and writing in religion and psychology to assist others in their personal development.

Notice that my goal statement contains no "job title." In other words, I am not saying who will *pay* me to do this. My goal could in fact be achieved as the pastor of a church, as an instructor in a college or university, as a professional writer, or as some combination of the above. While my goal statement does not specify who will pay me for performing this activity, it does, however, answer three basic questions:

Question	Answer
What is the *function* I want to perform?	Teaching and writing.
In what *occupational area* do I want to do this?	Religion and Psychology.
What is the *purpose* for which I want to do this?	To assist others in their personal development.

Examples of other similar goal statements have included the following:

—to create high quality hand-crafted furniture in my own shop, in a small town or rural area.

—to work with preschool children, in a setting that encourages their personal, social, and academic development.

—to be engaged in the financial operations of a small to medium size company that is experiencing rapid growth, and that is located in the western portion of the United States.

Now write your own goal statement. Once you have done that, put it away for a few days. Allow your mind to gain some perspective on what you have written. Then, when you are ready, take it out and make whatever changes or modifications you feel you need to make. When you are satisfied that your goal statement accurately describes what you would really like to accomplish, then you are ready to begin the second step in your career exploration, namely, to:

Identify an Occupation That Corresponds to Your Goal

To do this, go to your local library and, in the reference section, locate the latest edition of the *Occupational Outlook Handbook.*[1] This volume, published by the U.S. government, lists 250 occupations employing 95 percent of the United States work force. Look up the occupations that you believe might correspond to your goal statement in the "Index to Occupations" in the back of the book.

Take, for example, the woman who put down for her goal statement that she wanted "to work with preschool children, in a setting that encourages their personal, social, and academic development." She decided that *teaching* most closely described what she was interested in. Looking up "Teachers" in the index, she discovered separate listings for "Kindergarten and elementary school teachers," "Secondary school teachers," and "College and university faculty." Deciding that "Kindergarten and elementary school teachers" seemed closest to what she wanted to do, she read that article. She discovered that the article was arranged by title

according to the following categories:
—Nature of the work
—Working conditions / employment
—Places of employment
—Training, other qualifications, and advancement
—Job outlook
—Earnings
—Related occupations

A final selection, entitled "Sources for additional information," provided her with the names of national organizations in her field of interest, which could be contacted for additional information.

If the occupation she had been looking for had not been listed in the *Occupational Outlook Handbook,* she could have referred to the latest edition of another government publication, the *Dictionary of Occupational Titles,*[2] containing twenty thousand occupations, with information on each. This book also is available in the reference section of your local library.

These reference books, and others like them, are useful for translating your goal statement into the names of actual occupations in the real world. In the process of researching occupations, you may discover that what you said you wanted to do in your goal statement could actually be done in any one of several occupations. In that case, the question is, which of these occupations is the best for you. In order to find out, you need to:

Do an Informational Interview

An informational interview[3] is simply sitting down with someone who is doing the kind of work you are interested in and asking them what it is like to work in that particular career area. If you already know someone who is doing the kind of work you are interested in, call that person and ask if you can see him or her. If you don't personally know someone like this, look in the Telephone Yellow Pages under the business heading that corresponds to your area of interest, or speak to your pastor and ask if anyone in the church is engaged in this line of work. Then call or write an individual working in one of the companies or organizations doing the kind of work you want to know more about. Ask for a specified amount of that person's time. Ten minutes is good. When you see

the person, ask four basic questions:
—How did you get into this line of work?
—What do you like about this work?
—What don't you like about it?
—Who else could I talk to who does this same kind of work?
At the end of your ten minutes, thank the person for the time and get up and leave. Only stay beyond your allotted time if you are invited to do so. After your interview, write a thank-you note to the person, expressing your appreciation for the time given to you and stating how useful the talk was in allowing you to clarify your career goals.

Immediately after seeing this person, write down everything you remember about the conversation. Write down your first impressions of the nature of the work. Jot down any factual information the person gave you—names of national organizations in the field, other people to contact, and so forth. Ask yourself, do you enjoy doing the same kinds of things this person does? If so, you may be well suited to work in the same occupational area. Above all, were you really "turned on" by what you heard about the nature of the work? Sometimes the spark just isn't there, and you should know this *before* you make plans to enter this particular career field.

The most valuable thing about an informational interview is the chance to "reality check" *your* impressions of an occupational area against how it is actually experienced by someone working in it. The story is told of one woman who had always wanted to work in a doctor's office. After succeeding in getting hired as a doctor's receptionist and working in the office for a few weeks, she found herself becoming very depressed at dealing all day with people who were ill, people who didn't want to be there, who were afraid of seeing the doctor, and so forth. The point is, if she had done informational interviews with several doctor's receptionists *before* she got this job, her unpleasant surprise about the nature of the work could have been prevented.

Continue with your informational interviewing until you feel that you have narrowed down your occupational goal to *exactly* what it is you want to do.

A brief review: By this time you have
—expressed in general terms what you want to do by writing your personal *goal statement.*
—identified an occupation that corresponds to your goal by

researching possible occupations in the *Occupational Outlook Handbook* and *The Dictionary of Occupational Titles.*

—gotten a feel of what it is like to actually do the work you have in mind by doing several *informational interviews.*

When you believe you have discovered exactly what it is you want to do, there is one final issue you need to explore, and that is to:

Find Out What Is Holding You Back

The road to achieving any goal is seldom smooth. Inevitably, you will encounter roadblocks. Even if you firmly believe you are following God's direction for your life, natural fear or hesitation or even particular life circumstances may seem to stand in your way. On the other hand, there will be other factors working in your favor, even if it is only your strong desire to achieve your goal. It is important for you to identify what it is that is holding you back— and also what it is that is working in your favor— in order to increase the chances that you will succeed in achieving your goal. For this it will be helpful to do a *force field analysis.*

Take a piece of paper and write down your occupational goal in a box in the center of the sheet, as in the example on the next page. Then, to each side of the box, write down as many positive or negative factors as you can think of that are working either in favor or against your achieving your goal. Draw arrows of varying length to signify the relative strength of each positive or negative factor impinging on your goal.

For example, earlier in this chapter I cited the example of the man who expressed as his goal statement, "to create high quality hand-crafted furniture in my own shop, in a small town or rural area." This man summarized his occupational goal as "to own and operate a hand-crafted furniture shop." When he was done listing factors working both for and against his achieving his goal by means of doing a force field analysis, his result was the diagram reproduced on the next page.

By doing a force field analysis of his occupational goal, this man discovered that, although he had problems to overcome, such as lack of start-up capital and limited business experience, he also had

Force Field Analysis

Occupational Goal

Positives		Negatives

Positives

Strong interest in hand-crafted furniture.

——————————▶

Love working with my hands.

——————————▶

Strong desire to have my own business.

——————————▶

Strong personal motivation (hate present job).

——————————▶

Wife and kids highly supportive.

——————————▶

Brother-in-law runs own business (could get advice).

——————————▶

Start-up capital available from equity in house.

Goal

To own

and

operate

a

hand-

crafted

furniture

shop

Negatives

Time demands of present job make it hard for me to get started.

◀——————————

Fear of failure (I am scared!).

◀——————————

Limited business experience.

◀——————————

Expense of starting up a new business.

◀——————————

hidden assets, such as equity to borrow against and a brother-in-law who could advise him in business. The force field analysis also helped him get in touch with his strong emotional motivation for achieving his goal, reflected in his love of fine furniture and of working with his hands, as well as his lifelong desire to have his own business.

Probably the most valuable outcome of doing a force field analysis is that it gives you an opportunity to clearly identify the obstacles that seem to be standing in your way. Only when you see exactly what is holding you back can you begin to take steps to eliminate those obstacles. Begin by identifying the strongest negative factors working against achieving your goal, and then take steps to deal with these first. This man saw, for example, that the strongest obstacle to achieving his goal was that, since he was currently employed full-time on another job, he had little time to put into starting up a new business. Once he clearly identified this as his number one obstacle, he could begin to think of possible solutions. Among these would be reducing his hours at work and using this extra time to plan the new business or possibly saving money over a period of time to make it possible for him to quit his present job and give full-time to starting his own business. The point is, this problem—and others like it—are solvable in a variety of ways, but first we must see clearly what the problem *is* before we begin to take steps toward solving it.

In this chapter you have worked toward defining your vocation and identifying your occupational goal. You have identified occupations consistent with your goal and also factors working both in favor as well as against achieving it. At this point you are probably considering whether you have the necessary qualifications to achieve it. You are thinking: I know I want to work in graphic arts . . . or computers . . . or public relations . . . or counseling . . . but I have no *qualifications*. How can I get anyone to take me seriously?

In the next chapter we will discuss the subject of job qualifications and identify several strategies for gaining the qualifications you need.

Chapter Six

Step Four—
Assess Your
Qualifications

By now you should have a pretty good idea of what it is you want to do. Maybe you can *see* in your mind's eye that business you want to start . . . that counseling center you want to develop . . . that job in your present place of employment that you want to be offered. You have identified your occupational goal, and you believe it is consistent with your vocation as you understand it.

"But I'm not qualified," you say. "What good is knowing what God wants me to do when nobody is going to let me do it?"

Hold it right there! You may be more qualified than you think.

In discussing the qualifications for any job or career, it is important to realize that there are basically only four qualifications you must possess in order to be competitive. Three of these four can be acquired if you don't already possess them. The fourth you must possess before even considering the job or occupation for yourself (more on this later). The four basic qualifications for any job or career are:

—*Skills qualifications.* The ability to perform the tasks required, along with any special knowledge needed.
—*"Paper" qualifications.* Necessary licenses, credentials, permits, or academic degrees.
—*Experience qualifications.* A track record of having performed, successfully, the same or similar kind of work in the past.
—*Temperamental qualifications.* The type of personality that would

be happy and fulfilled doing the kind of work you have in mind.

To repeat, there are only four possible qualifications that are required for any job or career you may be considering. Knowing this makes it possible to figure out exactly which qualifications you already possess—and which you still lack—in order for you to do what you want to do.

Think now for a moment about your occupational goal. If you have not already written an occupational goal statement, sit down right now and write one. Go back to chapter five to see how to do this. Once you have written out a goal statement, keep it in mind as you read this chapter. As you read, consider in your own mind which qualifications you already possess to do what you want to do—and which you still need to acquire.

The first and most obvious of the four basic qualifications are:

Skills Qualifications

One of the most amazing success stories in recent college basketball was that of Zack Lieberman, a five foot, three-and-one-half inch guard on the team of the United States International University in San Diego.[1] One of the smallest college basketball players in America, Lieberman competed in a sport dominated by players six foot six. "The way I see it, his court savvy, ball-handling, and leadership ability washes away any liabilities he might have..." Lieberman's coach remarked. Lieberman is an example of a person with such highly developed *skills* qualifications that they more than make up for a possible lack of qualifications in other areas.

Skills qualifications may be the ball-handling ability of the professional athlete or the highly trained, technical skills of a brain surgeon. Or they may be of a more general nature, such as the "people skills" of a successful salesperson.

In order to find out what skills qualifications the occupation in which you are interested requires, go to your local library. Look up the occupation in *Occupational Outlook Handbook*,[2] found in the reference section of the library. Read especially the portion of the article entitled, "Nature of the Work." Following this, do an informational interview with someone actually working in this occupation. (Informational interviews were described in chapter five.) Finally, if you want a more detailed assessment of your abilities as they relate to the skills qualifications needed for a particular job or career, go to a college or university career counseling office or to a private career counselor and ask to be given an aptitude test, such as The Career Ability Placement Survey.[3] Your results on a test such as this will suggest areas in which you may need additional training in order to be competitive with people already working in the job or career you are considering.

Finally, a word of caution. Skills qualifications *alone* are not a sufficient reason for choosing to enter a particular job or occupation. The ranks of the *misemployed* are filled with individuals who chose their job or career because they possessed the skills qualifications for it but, as it turned out, they didn't possess the slightest interest in doing the work! Possessing skills qualifications is simply one of the ingredients in job satisfaction.

In order to work at a particular job or career, you must not only possess the *ability* to do it, that is, the skills qualifications. You must be *allowed* to do it! You need, in other words, to possess the right.

"Paper" Qualifications

"Paper" qualifications come in a variety of forms. Some paper qualifications are the licenses and certificates that are *legally* required to work in certain occupational areas. Try practicing medicine without a license, for example! Other paper qualifications are the educational requirements that employers require for certain jobs. You need to be a high school graduate to be considered for certain positions, a college or even graduate school graduate for others. Don't think that just because you may want to work for yourself that there are no paper qualifications required. In many states you must be licensed to provide home child care, for example.

To find out what paper qualifications you need for what you want to do, read "Training, Other Qualifications and Advancement" in *Occupational Outlook Handbook*. To find out what paper qualifications are required by a particular employer, simply ask the employer, the personnel officer, or some knowledgeable person already working in the company and doing the work you want to do.

A lot of people who are changing careers, or who are entering the work force for the first time, fall into the trap of thinking that they need elaborate paper qualifications in order to be employed in the field of their choice. They spend large amounts of time and money going back to school for retraining, sometimes unnecessarily. Often a person can be hired in a new field if he or she can demonstrate to the employer that he or she possesses a combination of *skills* qualifications and *experience* qualifications, even if they lack some of the usual *paper* qualifications. A general rule of thumb is, go back to school and retrain *only* if you have determined that it is absolutely necessary, *or* if you simply desire to build additional competence in a field for its own sake and/or for your own interest.

In some circumstances, however, it *will* make sense for you to go back to school. How can you handle the time and money involved in reschooling, especially if you are already working full-time at another job? Here are some options you might consider.

—Obtain a degree from the increasing number of colleges and universities that grant credit for *life experience*, that is, for previous employment in the field for which you desire the degree. See the chapter footnotes for the name of a national directory that lists schools that grant credit for life experience.[4]

—Enroll in a college or university *external degree* program (not to be confused with a "mail order" degree). In external degree programs you study at home, using materials the school sends you. Make sure the program is accredited and that you possess the necessary self-discipline to study at home.

—Enroll in a local college or university that offers a flexible class schedule tailored for working adults. An increasing number of colleges and universities have recognized the importance of the adult market in education and have scheduled classes for the convenience of working adults.

—Enroll in a vocational school specializing in training people for placement in the particular field you wish to enter.

—If you have decided that what you need is simply additional knowledge in a certain subject area and not an academic degree, then simply register for seminars and workshops in your area of interest. One man, the author of a best-selling book on self-employment, became an expert on this subject simply by attending workshops on self-employment over a two-year period.[5]

Finally, if you desire to enter a certain field of employment and do not possess the required paper qualifications for entrance at the top rungs of this field, consider earning the paper qualifications for *alternative* roles in the same field. Suppose you always wanted to be a medical doctor, for example, but never completed the necessary education. How about considering such positions within the medical field as physician assistant, medical assistant, emergency medical technician, physical therapist, or psychiatric-mental health technician? Granted, these all have their *own* paper qualifications. But the qualifications for these positions are less exhaustive than those required of a medical doctor. And working in one of these alternative roles would give you the opportunity to work in a responsible position in the field of your choice—medicine. Other professions, such as law, have similar paraprofessional roles. Brouse around in the *Occupational Outlook Handbook* to see which alternative roles in the profession of your choice appeal to you. Then get to work to acquire the paper qualifications for those alternative positions.

Experience Qualifications

If you think you are "unqualified," it is probably this area of qualifications that you are thinking of. Also, there is a Catch-22 here. An employer won't consider you if you have no experience. On the other hand, how can you *get* experience if no one will hire you?

The first thing to do is ask yourself, is it really true that you have no experience doing this—or something *like* this? If the job you are applying for is something you like doing (which it should be, or you shouldn't be applying for it), then it is extremely unlikely that you have done nothing like this previously, even if you have been out of the paid work force for twenty years. Is the job one where you meet the public and deal with people on a friendly basis? How about relating some of your previous *volunteer* activities to this?

Does the job involve working in a high-pressure situation while managing people effectively? How about the pressure you experience and the people management skills you develop while raising children? The point is, your previous experience does not have to be *paid* to count as *work*. Many of your involvements in the church may have demonstrated skills and abilities similar to those you would use in the career of your choice. What you have to do is present your previous experience *as* work—and especially, as work related to exactly the kind of thing you desire to be doing. This is where a well written résumé comes in. (We will discuss résumés in chapter eight of this book.)

Suppose, however, that you truly have not done any work similar to what you are applying for, *or* that your prospective employers simply do not buy your previous experience as "real work." There are still ways of *getting* the experience you need:

—*Volunteering*. Volunteering can be used to *gain* experience in a field of your choice and then, if you desire, to use this experience as a way of transitioning into paid employment in that same field. We will discuss some of the details of how this can be done in the next chapter. Sunday newspapers in some cities have a special section on volunteer opportunities in the community. Your church offers a multitude of volunteer opportunities, some of them undoubtedly in your area of interest. Decide which opportunities in your church or community correspond to your area of interest. Then get to work to *acquire* the experience you lack through volunteer service.

—*Internships*. Some employers offer internships, in which people interested in a particular field earn while they learn. The more able interns are often hired for a permanent position by their former training employers. Other internships, probably the majority, are not paid but do provide an opportunity to gain experience in the field of your choice, in preparation for later securing a paid position in this same field. Find out what internships are available in your field of interest, and what are the qualifications for entering these programs, by consulting guides on internship opportunities, such as the two listed in the chapter notes.[6]

—*On-the-job training*. If you demonstrate interest and ability for a certain type of work, an employer will sometimes hire you to do the job and then train you in the specific work procedures you need to know. In this case you have the best of all worlds—the opportunity to learn more about the kind of work in which you are interested, and to be paid for it at the same time.

One should never allow oneself to be stopped from achieving a goal simply because one "lacks experience." If you *do* lack experience, *acquire* it—and get on with your career and your life.

Temperamental Qualifications

Up to now we have been talking about qualifications that, if you didn't already have them, you could get. Skills qualifications can usually be learned. Paper qualifications can be earned. Experience qualifications can be acquired. Temperamental qualifications, however, are *inherent*. That is, you either have them or you don't. They are based on the nature of the personality that God has given you. Therefore, it is important to know *before* you make plans to enter a particular job or career whether or not you have the temperamental qualifications for it.

What are temperamental qualifications? They are those temperamental characteristics that make you suited, or not suited, for certain occupations, based upon the needs and preferences of the personality that was formed in you as a child or that, to some extent, you may even have been born with. Some characteristics of temperament were described in chapter three. They include such characteristics as the degree to which you prefer to work alone or with others, whether you tend to be emotionally oriented or more objective in your thinking, and whether you are firm-minded and decisive or more flexible and open-minded in your thinking. As we suggested in chapter three, particular *aspects* of your temperament may alter over time. A person in an executive position, for example, may *learn* to be more decisive, or a basically introverted person may develop more tolerance for working with many people on a daily basis. However, while particular temperamental characteristics may alter over time, the basic *pattern* of your temperament remains remarkably consistent throughout life. Therefore it makes sense to follow this general principle when choosing a job or career: *Choose a job or career consistent with the nature of your temperamental qualifications.* Do not attempt to *bend* your temperament in order to fit the requirements of a particular job or career.

How can you judge your own temperamental qualifications for a particular job? Ask yourself some common sense questions, such as those listed in the "Now I Want to Ask Myself" section of chapter three. Then go back to the *Occupational Outlook Handbook.* Read the description of the job or career that interests you. Compare the demands of this job or career with what you know of your own temperamental preferences. Ask yourself if the two seem compatible. Do an informational interview with some people working in the field you are considering, to see whether your impressions of a particular career correspond to the reality of what it is like actually to do this work.

Finally, if you want more detailed information about whether your temperament is suited to a particular job or career, make an appointment with a county or state employment assistance office, with your college or university career planning and placement office, or with a private counselor, and ask to be given a personality assessment inventory. One of these is the Myers-Briggs Types Indicator, discussed in chapter three. Other instruments are also commonly used by counselors to assess a client's suitability for various occupations. After you have taken one or more of these tests, ask your counselor's opinion of your temperamental qualifications for the job or occupation you may be considering.

Assessing Your Qualifications

Now is the time to look at your own qualifications and decide which you need in order to achieve your occupational goal. Remember, if you don't have one or more of the qualifications, you can *acquire* them, with the exception of temperamental qualifications, which you must possess in order to consider entering a particular job or occupation in the first place. On pages 76 and 77 is a Qualifications Checklist, compiled as by a woman whose occupational goal is to own and operate her own catering business. Read it over. Use it as a model for writing your *own* Qualifications Checklist, to assist you in clarifying exactly the qualifications you need to transform your occupational goal into an achieved reality.

Let's Review the Steps

In this book I suggest that achieving career satisfaction and success is a five-step process.

—*Step one*: Understand your personality.
—*Step two*: Have some crazy dreams.
—*Step three*: Focus on a goal.
—*Step four*: Assess your qualifications.

We are now ready to discuss the fifth and last step in the process, which is to identify who is going to pay you to do what you want to do. In the next chapter we will talk about employment and discuss four ways to express your vocation by means of a job, a career, or volunteer service.

Qualifications Checklist

Occupational *Goal*	to run my own catering business, employing at least three people, including myself, and specializing in catering dinners and parties in private homes.
Target Date	November 15, 1989

Qualifications Needed	Qualifications I Still Lack	Battle Plan	Target Date
Skills Qualifications			
-food preparation and handling -supervisory and management skills -bookkeeping	- bookkeeping	-complete bookkeeping course	-1/30/89 course completion
Paper Qualifications			
-2 yr. college culinary arts program -business license -health certificate	-completion of program -business license -health certificate	-complete education -acquire bus. license -take physical exam	-5/30/89 completed -1/6/89 applied for -1/25/89 scheduled
Experience Qualifications			
-six months assisting an established caterer	-another three months working for present employer	-complete three more months with present employer	-6/15/89 completion of 6 mos. w/present employer

Temperamental Qualifications

-extraverted personality
-true liking for people
-ability to function under pressure
-creative flair
-entrepreneurial drive

Making Out Your Qualifications Checklist
(Please refer to the chart on the opposite page.)

Occupational Goal

Be specific. The more specific you are in describing exactly what it is you want to achieve, the more clearly you will be able to determine what qualifications are needed, and the more motive power you will have to achieve your goal.

Target Date

Again, be specific. Nail it down! This is the date by which you intend to achieve your occupational goal, as described above.

Qualifications Needed

(Column 1) Include the qualifications that are *legally* required, mainly under paper qualifications, as well as whatever skills and experience qualifications are wise to have in order to achieve your occupational goal. When listing temperamental qualities, be honest. If you believe that you lack one or more of the temperamental qualifications for your goal, you would be wise to either change or alter your occupational goal in accord with the temperamental qualifications you do possess.

Qualifications I Still Lack

(Column 2) List qualifications from column 1 that you do not currently possess.

Battle Plan

(Column 3) Describe how you are going to acquire the needed qualifications listed in column 2.

Target Date

(Column 4) Write the completion dates of the various strategies you cited under Battle Plan in Column 3. By doing this you can coordinate the completion dates of all your needed qualifications as you move toward achieving your occupational goal.

Chapter Seven

Step Five—Go for It!

"Don't dream it. Be it."　　　　　　　　　—car bumper sticker

"As each has received a gift, employ it. . . ."　　　—1 Peter 4:10

In this chapter I am asking you to make one basic assumption. I am asking you to *assume* that you are going to achieve the occupational goal you have set for yourself. The question therefore is not *whether* you are going to achieve your goal. The question is *how*. In this chapter I am going to help you identify a strategy that will enable you to achieve your goal and express the vocation to which God is calling you.

Before we begin, take a moment to do the puzzle on page 79. The idea is to connect all nine dots by means of four straight, unbroken lines without taking your pencil off the page. Try it. The solution is on page 80 but please— no peeking! When you think you have the solution, or you give up, turn to page 80 for your answer.

As you can see, the solution involves going outside the imaginary box defined by the outer row of dots. "I didn't know you could do that," you say. Why not? Where in the directions did I say you had to stay inside the box? The point is, when we are thinking about how we might achieve our occupational goal, we tend to limit ourselves by imagining rules that don't necessarily exist. We literally box ourselves in. Often the creative solution to achieving what we want to achieve is found *outside* the circumscribed area we thought existed.

In this chapter we are going to look at some creative solutions to achieving your occupational goal.

•   •   •

•   •   •

•   •   •

Whether you feel God is calling you to teach preschool, develop an interior decorating business, or build a better mousetrap, there are basically only four possible ways of doing it. You can:

—*Do it where you are.* Look at your present job, assuming you are employed, and figure out how you can make changes in your current responsibilities so that you can do what you want to do right where you are. This is *job restructuring.*

—*Do it somewhere else.* You decide that, in order for you to do what you want to do, you must completely change your environment. This is *job or career change.*

—*Do it for yourself.* You decide that the best way to do what you want to do is to start your own business. This is *self-employment.*

—*Do it for free.* You decide to give your work away, either because you simply enjoy doing it, or because you hope to gain valuable experience to put toward paid employment later. This is *volunteering.*

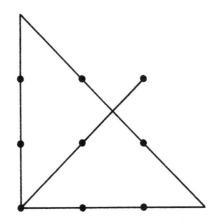

To repeat, anything you might want to do, any vocation you believe God is calling you to, can be accomplished by means of one or more of these four ways. What you must decide is, which one is the *best* way for you to achieve your goal. To help you decide, we will now look at the four ways in more detail. As we do so, I want you to be thinking of which of these would be the best strategy for you to begin to achieve your occupational goal and to live out the vocation to which God is calling you.

Do It Where You Are: Job Restructuring

Richard Bolles points out that every job has some degree of "space."[1] By "space" he means the freedom a particular job allows to do the job the way the employee sees fit, or to incorporate into that job elements that had not been part of it before. Let's look at two very different examples of job "space."

Our first example is that of a semi-skilled worker in an auto assembly plant. Every seventeen seconds a car chassis moves down the assembly line. Our imaginary worker tightens two bolts on the fender, one bolt on the left and another on the right. By the time he finishes with the second one, another chassis is moving down the line. Again he tightens two bolts, one on the left and another on the right. And so it goes, throughout the day.

How much "space" does our auto worker enjoy on the job? Practically none. He is limited by the *time* constraints of this particular job. He is also limited by the *task* requirements of the job. Those bolts have to be tightened. If he feels a calling, for example, to assist his co-workers with their personal problems, obviously this is something he will have to do completely *off* the job.

Now let us take another example, one that I am familiar with from my own professional background in the church ministry. Let us imagine the minister of the local church decides that what she really wants to do is to counsel people. She feels called to work with others on a one-to-one basis and assist them in working through troublesome areas of their lives. My guess is that she could do this as much as twenty hours a week and still accomplish all the necessary business of the church—writing sermons, calling on people in the hospital, and administering the church. If we figure that our imaginary minister works perhaps a fifty-hour week, that means that the "space" allowed for her particular job is about forty percent of the total time, or about twenty hours a week. And this "space" could be used for other pursuits besides counseling, depending upon her own interests. She could start a school in the church, expand the music program, or initiate a liturgical drama group. The point is, church ministry is an example of a job that offers considerable "space," and that consequently easily lends itself to *job restructuring*.

Not all of us are in the happy situation where we can so easily restructure our existing job. Most of us operate somewhere between our imaginary factory worker and the minister cited above. What you need to do is to look at your present job and compare what you are *paid* to do with what you *want* to do. Read over your occupational goal statement that you wrote for the last chapter. Ask yourself, does that particular thing need to be done—or is it already being done by somebody else—right where you work? If so, consider whether you could:

—negotiate with your boss to allow you to take on some of that same kind of work as part of your present job, *or*

—use your present job as a base to move *within* the company to where the kind of work you are interested in doing is being done.

One woman who did this successfully was interested in working in graphic arts, even though her present job with the company was in another area entirely. This woman approached her boss with the request that she spend a portion of her time working in graphic arts. The boss agreed. Over a period of time she was able to build up this area of involvement and, at the same time, negotiate with her boss and co-workers to reduce her work load in other areas. The end result was that she was finally employed by this same company *entirely* in graphic arts—the area where she really wanted to be in the first place! What she did, you may be able to do as well. Look at your present employment. Ask yourself, "Could I begin to do what I want to do where I work right now?"

There are employment situations, however, that simply do not allow the opportunity for you to do what you really want to do. In situations like these, your best bet may be to:

Do It Somewhere Else: Job or Career Change

A recent article in a national publication profiled individuals who had made dramatic changes in their jobs or careers and who were thriving in their new professions:[2]

—a former New York trial lawyer, now running a membership service company specializing in performing household tasks for busy working people
—another former lawyer, a specialist in environmental issues, now running a school to teach people to build their own environment-respecting houses
—a former physician, now working as an investment counselor
—a former college dean, now serving as sales executive for a resort on the East Coast
—a former research chemist, now enjoying new work as a career counselor

Job or career changes such as those cited above are possible because all of us possess what career counselors call *transferable skills*. These are simply skills we use in our present employment that we could "transfer" to another kind of employment. Making a career switch involves becoming aware of what our transferable skills are—and where they could be used in another line of work. Changing jobs or careers involves making use of the commonly used tools of the trade. These include the résumé, letters of recommendation, and interviewing. We will discuss these in the next chapter. Changing jobs or careers also involves choosing a particular *strategy* that will work for you. For some it may be volunteering in order to gain experience in a new line of work. Others may acquire an internship. Some imaginative souls will invent their own job, and convince a would-be employer to pay them to do it!

One person who invented her own job was Lainie Carter, at the time a 55-year-old grandmother and former doctor's receptionist in San Diego, California, who became concerned with the number of parents of newborn babies who needed training in parenting skills during the first few months of their new baby's life.[3] Lainie approached Scripps Memorial Hospital in San Diego with the suggestion that the hospital hire her to work with these parents. The result: Lainie Carter was hired as the "new family consultant" at Scripps Hospital. Commonly referred to as Scripps' "surrogate grandmother," Carter had probably the only job of its kind in the country when she began.

For those who would like to know more about inventing their own job, Richard Bolles' and John Crystal's *Where Do I Go from Here with My Life?* contains useful guidelines for presenting a job proposal to a would-be employer.[4]

Some people, however, may not want to work for anybody else at all. For these independent souls, even a self-invented job may prove too confining. For them, the solution may be to:

Do It for Yourself: Self-Employment

Ah, the dream of being your own boss! Owning your own resort hotel in the Poconos, building up your own retail business, doing your own *thing*—at your own pace, in your own style, with nobody to answer to but yourself.

Starting your own business is an option. Approximately six hundred thousand people do it every year. But before you take the plunge, there are some things you should know.

First, the statistics are not encouraging. According to the Small

Business Administration, 50 percent of all new businesses do not survive past the fifth year.[5] An article in a national publication states that, of the estimated sixteen hundred new businesses started in our country every day, fourteen hundred and eighty will eventually fail.[6]

Second, it takes a particular personality to be successful as an entrepreneur. Among the traits needed are the ability to set goals and stick to them, the willingness to take calculated risks, and a tendency to admire others who control their own destinies. It is probably fair to say that most of us need the emotional security of a paycheck coming in from somebody *else* every month!

Third, going into business for yourself is not for those whose work habits are such that they simply can't make it working for somebody else. If anything, your work habits need to be *better* than average if you are self-employed. It is likely that you will work *longer* hours, for *less* pay—at least at first—than the person who works for somebody else.

Having said all this, the fact remains that self-employment and entrepreneurship may be the wave of the future. John Naisbitt cites this as one of the "megatrends" currently shaping our society.[7] Self-employment is also a particularly attractive option for women, both for those who continue to encounter sex discrimination in the workplace, as well as for those who seek a flexible work schedule by working at their own business out of their homes. According to the U.S. Labor Department, from 1970 to 1983, the number of self-employed women increased five times faster than the number of self-employed men.[8]

If you are thinking of starting your own business, the question is, what *kind* of business. Identifying self-employment as your occupational goal is like saying you are planning to take your vacation in a Chevy—you have identified the vehicle but not the destination! Many self-employed people succeed only in buying their own job. If that will be the case with you, the job should be something you enjoy doing in the first place. If you are planning to spend all day watering and caring for plants in connection with your own indoor nursery service for restaurants, public buildings, and private homes, then you'd better enjoy working with plants all day! The point is, self-employment is simply one *vehicle* for doing a particular thing. Your question still is, *what* is it that you want to do? If, however, you feel you do know what you want to do, and you are the kind of person who can deal, temperamentally, with a degree of risk-taking, then self-employment may be the way to go. Test the waters before you take the plunge. Start your business part-time and see how it goes. Take advantage of the expert advice of others. In many cities, an organization named SCORE (Service Corps of Retired Executives) will give free advice on starting and operating your own small business.

There is still one more option for doing what you want to do. This option may be used as an end in itself, or it may be used as a vehicle for moving from one career to another. It is to:

Do It for Free: Volunteering

Don't laugh! If you simply want to get involved in a particular activity for the fun of it, or if you want to test out an alternative line of work, or for a number of other reasons, volunteering may be the way to go.

First of all, let's lay to rest the myth that volunteering means doing the simple-minded tasks that nobody else will take on. The fact is, volunteering involves doing every kind of activity that people also get paid to do. We have two work forces in this country—one paid and the other volunteer—and everything that people do for pay other people do for free. In 1985 alone, nearly 90 million Americans volunteered time worth an estimated dollar value of $100 billion.[9] Your church and your community provide countless opportunities for volunteer service, in which you can develop your skills and help others at the same time.

Why would anyone work for free instead of for pay? Here are some reasons:

—*For the joy of it.* For someone who doesn't need to be compensated financially for their work, or for one whose paid job doesn't allow them to express certain aspects of themselves, volunteering gives them a chance to do what they really want to do, while at the same time possibly helping others. This may be especially important at midlife, when heretofore unexpressed aspects of ourselves cry out for recognition and satisfaction.

—*To gain experience.* Kitti Johnson, a San Diego, California, radio personality, volunteered for three years as a team member of a religious television program before beginning her paid career in broadcasting. Alden Lancaster volunteered through her church to work with refugees in Thailand before accepting a paid position directing refugee resettlement services for a church agency in San Diego. Kitti and Alden are examples of many people whose volunteer work led to paid employment in the same area of involvement.

—*To "test the waters."* You think you would like to get into a certain line of work, but you are not sure. Volunteering is a low-risk way to find out. If you try it and find you don't like it, what have you lost? Better this way than to invest a couple of years and thousands of dollars in training for a field that you later discover you don't want to be in.

—*To make contacts.* Volunteering allows you to meet people with your same interests, people who are already doing what you would like to do. If the time should come that you wish to transition into paid employment in this same area of activity, you have already made some contacts in the field.

—*To stretch yourself.* A lot of people don't realize that volunteering actually allows an individual to start at a higher level of responsibility than they would be able to if they were paid for the same work. For four years I served as a volunteer team member of a religious television show. I conducted interviews on the air, including one with former Secretary of State Cyrus Vance. I wonder how many years it would have taken me to be allowed to do interviews of this caliber if I had been a paid television broadcaster. As a volunteer, I was able to "jump right in!"

There are also, obviously, disadvantages to volunteering:

—*No money.* Nobody is paying you to do this. Unfortunately, not everybody can give of time without the expectation of financial remuneration.

—*Time and energy commitments.* Even though you are working for free, volunteering takes time and energy. You need to balance the demands of your volunteer work with those of your paid employment, as well as those of your family.

—*Possible lack of credibility.* There is still some tendency for others, including prospective employers, not to give equal value to a person's volunteer work experience. One way to overcome this is to describe your volunteer work in commonly accepted professional language when you are applying for a job. I can think of one woman who presented her volunteer work in public relations so successfully that she was offered a paid public relations position in a hospital. After a few years in this position she left for a paid public relations position in a private school. It can be done!

In conclusion, volunteering has its advantages and disadvantages. If you are clear in your own mind about why you want to volunteer, and about *what* you expect to get out of it, then volunteering can be a rewarding experience.

Possibly the biggest advantage of volunteering, however, is that, if you are entering the paid work force for the first time, or if you are changing careers into a field for which you have limited training or experience, volunteering may be not only the best but also, in some cases, almost the *only* way of breaking into the career of your choice. During the course of four years I moved from being a full-time minister in a local church to working half-time as a writer, editor, and radio and television broadcaster—this with no formal journalistic training and no previous experience in the field. The key to my success in breaking in was volunteering. I was willing, at first, to give my time away. If, during this transitional period, I had decided to change careers completely, my progression from working full-time in the communications field (my second career) could be diagrammed in this fashion:

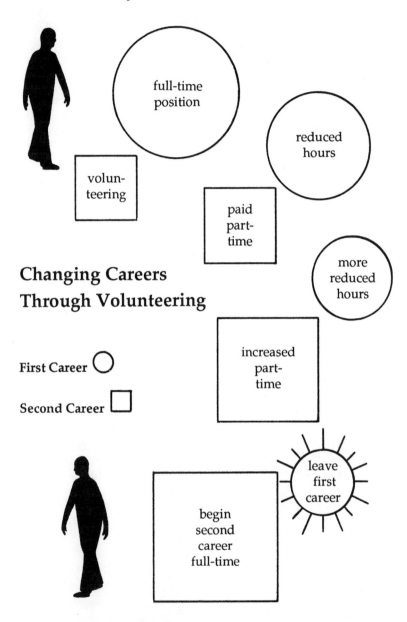

**Changing Careers
Through Volunteering**

First Career ◯

Second Career ☐

Again, volunteering may be about the *only* way for an individual to make the transition into a career for which that individual possesses (1) no formal training and (2) no previous work experience. If your present job is part-time, or has a flexible work schedule, you may gradually be able to cut back on the hours of your current job, as I did, while building up work involvement in your second career. If, on the other hand, you are tied to a forty-hour week in your current job, you will have to begin by involving yourself in your second career during your off-work hours—in other words, by moonlighting. Career transitions, as difficult as they may be, can be accomplished, and volunteering is often the key to starting the process.

Which Strategy Should I Use?

In this chapter we have looked at four strategies for enabling you to do what you want to do:

—*Strategy number one*—do it where you are: *job restructuring.*
—*Strategy number two*—do it somewhere else: *job or career change.*
—*Strategy number three*—do it for yourself: *self-employment.*
—*Strategy number four*—do it for free: *volunteering.*

The question of which strategy is right for you is best answered in the manner of the White Hare in *Alice in Wonderland*—it depends where you want to go! If, for example:

—You believe you can do what you want to right where you are working right now, by making some changes in your job description, then your best bet is *strategy number one*—do it where you are: *job restructuring.*
—You believe that doing what you want to do will involve a complete career change, or at the very least, a job change, then your solution is *strategy number two*—do it somewhere else: *job or career change.*
—You believe that no one else will give you a chance to do what you want to do exactly the way *you* want to do it, or you simply have an independent streak, then your solution is *strategy number three*—do it for yourself: *self-employment.*
—You don't care that much about being paid for what you enjoy doing, *or* you want to build expertise in a particular area in

preparation for eventual paid employment in that same area, then your solution is *strategy number four*—do it for free: *volunteering.*

You might also consider using more than one strategy in order to get where you finally want to go. Suppose, for example, that you are a secretary and you really want to get into accounting and nobody where you currently work will let you "try your wings." You might consider using *strategy number three: self-employment,* and start a small, free-lance accounting business in your home in your spare time and then, later, on the basis of this, go back to your present employer and present yourself as someone who has experience in accounting as demonstrated by your business. Or, you might consider *strategy number four: volunteering,* and volunteer to assist in the accounting department of your present employer on your own time, in order to "learn the ropes," or volunteer to assist with bookkeeping and accounting for volunteer groups in your community and then, later, apply for an accounting position with your present employer, presenting yourself as one who has experience in this area. In this example, you would have used *strategy number three: self-employment,* or *strategy number four: volunteering,* in the interests of *strategy number one: job restructuring.* The point is, there are many ways to achieve your occupational goal. Decide which way(s) suits you best—and then go for it!

In this section of the book we have used a five-step process to help you define the nature of your vocation and how it can be expressed by means of paid employment or volunteer service. We have shown how you can determine the needs of your own particular personality, and how you can get in touch with your interests, values, and abilities by means of several written exercises. In the next section of this book we will turn to the practical *how to*'s of getting hired for a job or career that's consistent with your vocation. The first of these is the résumé and the job recommendation, which we will look at in the next chapter.

Part Three

Practical Strategies That Make a Difference

Chapter Eight

Résumé and Recommendations— Taking Charge of Your "Paper Trail"

It is not enough simply to *be* qualified for a job. You must *prove* that you are qualified—by showing the employer what you have done in the past and what you are likely to do in the future. The tools for doing this are the résumé and job recommendations—your "paper trail" to successful job placement. In this chapter I will show you how to use these tools effectively to help you achieve your occupational goal and begin to express your vocation by means of paid employment.

The Résumé—What It Is and What It Isn't

People sometimes fail to write an effective résumé because they are not sure exactly what its purpose is or what it is supposed to look like. Actually, the easiest way to think of a résumé is this: It is simply a listing, usually on one page, of previous work experience, along with the education and training that led up to it.

The chart on the next two pages shows a sample résumé, based on the one I wrote for myself before I secured my present position. The different portions are labeled, showing the purpose of each.

There are several things to remember when writing your résumé:

93

What to Include on . . .

Keep this section simple. You want people to see at a glance how to contact you and what your phone number is. Don't clutter it up with a lot of extraneous information, such as your social security number or the name of your children.

Here some people put instead a section titled "Occupational Goal," in which they state in their own words the kind of position they are seeking (which is also, one hopes, the kind of position for which they are sending the résumé!).

Notice the reverse chronological order. The idea is that your most recent experience is the most important. This is the one that the person reading your résumé wants to see first.

Notice that I have listed two or more positions within the time noted by the years in the left-hand column. Usually each position is listed with the years for that *particular* position in the left-hand column. The way I have done it here, however, is useful in situations in which (1) you have had several part-time jobs within the same period, *or* (2) you have changed jobs frequently within a short period of time. You will notice, however, that I have noted the *exact* years for each job listed at the end of the job description.

This section can be used to list nonpaid work experience as well. These include volunteer involvements, leisure activities, and even homemaker roles. This is "work" too, right? Simply list these roles as you would any job, by title, years of activity, and responsibilities involved.

Again, reverse chronological order. This section can also contain education received even though the degree was not completed. It can also list nondegree education or training, such as short-term certificate programs, on-the-job training, and self-directed study.

Have you received awards or special recognitions, especially for work activities related to the kind of position for which you are applying? If not, skip this section.

Notice the references are not listed in this résumé. List them on a separate sheet and *keep* this sheet until the employer requests it, usually after the interview.

Your Résumé

Christopher C. Moore
1367 Somermont Drive
El Cajon, CA 92021

(619) 298-2130 - office
448-9281 - home

PROFESSION
Ordained minister (Episcopal), teacher, and communicator

EMPLOYMENT HISTORY

1979 - present   Assistant, St. Luke's Episcopal Church, San Diego, California, (1980–present).

Public Information Officer, San Diego County Ecumenical Conference and the Episcopal Diocese of San Diego, including responsibilities for Episcopal Community Services, (1979–83).

Associate, St. Alban's Episcopal Church and Administrator of the Parish Day School, El Cajon, California, (1979–81).

1974 - 1977   Rector, Grace Episcopal Church, Linden, New Jersey, and member of the Editorial Board of THE CHURCH NEWS: DIOCESE OF NEW JERSEY EDITION, (1977–78).

Assistant, Grace Episcopal Church, Merchantville, New Jersey, (1974–77).

1969 - 1971   Instructor (English and Journalism) at the Forman Schools, Litchfield, Connecticut, and free-lance writer for the LITCHFIELD INQUIRER, (1970–71).

Instructor (English) at the Englewood School for Boys, Englewood, New Jersey, (1969–70).

EDUCATION
Doctoral student, 1978–79, Humanistic Psychology Institute, San Francisco, California. (9 graduate credits completed).

M.Div., Andover Newton Theological School, Newton Centre, Massachusetts.

M.A., 1968, Drew University, Madison, New Jersey, in English and American Literature.

B.A., 1965, Muhlenberg College, Allentown, Pennsylvania, Humanities (English) Major.

AWARDS
EMMY, for excellence in religious broadcasting in the Religious Programs category, awarded by the National Association of Television Arts and Sciences, San Diego Chapter, to the FOCUS 5IVE television program, which I served as team member. May, 1981.

REFERENCES AVAILABLE UPON REQUEST

—*A résumé is not simply a work biography.* It is better understood as an *advertisement*—for yourself. Or rather, a résumé is an advertisement for yourself *masquerading* as a work biography.

—*A résumé is written from the point of view of the position for which you are applying.* This means that you emphasize previous work experience and training that relate to the nature of the position you are seeking, and de-emphasize experience and training that do not relate to this position. In other words, you do not ordinarily list that college summer job as a lifeguard when you are applying for the position of office manager.

—*A résumé must be well prepared.* To understand why, you must understand the purpose of a résumé from the *employer's* point of view. For the employer, the résumé is a way of weeding out job applicants. The résumé enables the employer to whittle down the thirty or forty people who have applied for the job to the five or six who will finally be interviewed. What this means for *you* is that, in order to keep *you* from being one of those who are eliminated, your résumé must be done with extreme care.

The Résumé and Special Circumstances

Suppose you have not been in the paid work force for twenty years and you are now going back to work. Or suppose you are applying for positions in two or three different occupational areas. How do you write a résumé to deal with these special circumstances?

For the person preparing to re-enter the work force, it is important to realize that you did not live in a vacuum during those years when you were "not working." In fact you were involved in a variety of activities, including perhaps even raising a family. These activities demonstrated skills and abilities, as well as areas of special interest. Present these in the form of a *functional* résumé. A functional résumé, as opposed to a chronological résumé, such as the one illustrated in this chapter, is simply one that lists skills and abilities and general *areas* of previous experience in place of a chronological job listing. When writing a functional résumé, it is wise to describe previous activities in commonly accepted professional language. A volunteer fund raiser for the Girl Scouts is a "development assistant," for example. To find out how to describe areas of your previous experience in language more commonly accepted in business or the professions, ask someone you know who is currently working in the type of field you wish to enter, or look up sample résumés in books in the career or business sections of your local library or bookstore.

If you are applying for jobs in two or three different occupational areas, you simply cannot write one general purpose résumé that will present you favorably for consideration in these different occupational areas. You must write one résumé for *each* of the different occupational areas you are trying to enter. Only by doing this will you appear to employers to be focused upon, and have the qualifications for, the particular occupational area that they represent and stand a good chance of getting hired in at least *one* of the areas you are considering.

A word of warning: Considering two or three different occupational areas may be a sign that you have not really narrowed down your job search to exactly what it is you want to do and what God is calling you to do. You may still be "hedging your bets" and putting responsibility for choosing an occupation into the hands of an employer. If you suspect that this may be true of you, go back and reread chapter five, "Focus on a Goal," and figure out *exactly* what it is you want to do. You may find that the need to apply in two or three different occupational areas disappears.

How to Use a Résumé

If it is true, as I said previously, that employers use résumés for the purpose of *eliminating* people from consideration, should you try to avoid using one entirely, or are there circumstances where using a résumé can work to your advantage? Here are some ways that the use of a résumé can help you:

As an aid in assembling job-related information. When you are filling out that job application for XYZ Company, or sitting for your interview with the company personnel director, you don't want to be groping around in your mind for exactly when it was that you worked for ABC Company, or what your job title was. What better way to get these facts clear in your mind *before* you begin your job search than to sit down and write a one-page chronological résumé for your own use? This way you have your basic information together where you can refer to it whenever needed. This basic résumé can also serve as a model when rewriting your résumé for special uses, as described below. If you have your résumé word-processed and on disk, future revisions can easily be made without the need to retype the entire résumé.

To follow up after the interview. Some career counselors suggest that the best time to hand in your résumé is *after* you have been interviewed for the position. By this time you know something about the position and can rewrite your résumé to relate to the requirements of this particular job. If you can get away with not handing in a résumé before your interview, send in your rewritten résumé as a follow-up to the interview, along with a cover letter expressing interest in the position for which you were interviewed.

When you have found your dream job. You can't believe it! You have read or heard about this fantastic position that is everything you always wanted in a job. Perhaps you have been interviewed for it. The sense of inner excitement that you feel about this job leads you to believe that it represents a way of living out the vocation to which God is calling you. You want this job so much you can *taste* it!

If you have not already handed in your résumé, go home and rewrite it just for this one particular position. Present yourself as the perfect person for this job by adapting your résumé to the requirements for this particular position. And do the same thing *every* time you are in contention for one of these "special" jobs that really turn you on.

"Wait a minute," you say. "You don't expect me to rewrite my résumé completely for *one* job, do you? It's such a hassle to write a résumé *once*. Now I'm supposed to rewrite it every time I hear about a job that really turns me on?"

Look at it this way. Special jobs that are almost exactly suited to your own particular interests and abilities don't come along every day. Suppose you did this five times during the course of your job search. And suppose you had a success rate of one in five. That means you would be hired for exactly the job you always wanted. Isn't it worth going to some extra trouble, if it succeeds in getting you exactly the position you were always looking for—the position that allows you to express your real vocation?

Getting Good Job Recommendations

After your résumé, recommendations are the second part of your "paper trail" to landing a new job. They can be written, at your request, by a former boss for a prospective employer. They can also be given over the phone by a former boss to the hiring officer of the company you are applying to. Generally, you request recommendations from people you have worked for in the past, or at least of friends and acquaintances who know your abilities well enough to comment intelligently on the strengths you would bring to a new job.

Your first decision is whom to select. This is an important consideration, especially for those who have been out of the work force for some time. That next-door neighbor may be a wonderful friend. But can she really say anything about your abilities that would sound convincing to an employer? So your first rule is, select people who can speak intelligently about your abilities as they relate to the demands of the position for which you are applying.

Once you have decided whom you are going to ask for recommendations, be sure to ask if they are willing to do this. Then, give them enough information —both about the job for which you are applying and also about your qualifications for it—so that they can do a creditable job. Let me give three examples to show why this is important.

Example One. Your former boss, Mr. Rogers, of ABC Company, is sitting in his office. Suddenly the phone rings.

"Mr. Rogers?"

"Yes. . . ."

"This is Tom Jones of XYZ Company. I'd like to ask you a few questions about Mary Reynolds, who used to work for you. She has given your name as a reference."

"Mary Reynolds? Mary Reynolds. . . . I don't think I remember. . . . Oh, wait a minute! Yes, Mary Reynolds. I think she did work here. Wasn't in back in '82?"

The fact is, if you were Mary Reynolds, you would already have blown your recommendation. You would have blown it by not informing your former boss that you had given his name as a reference. And you would have blown it by not giving him information—both about you and also about the nature of the new job—so that he could speak convincingly about you to Mr. Jones.

Now let's imagine how this could have been handled better.

Example Two. Again, Mr. Rogers, your former boss, is sitting in his office. This time he has on his desk a note from you, asking if he would be willing to be your reference for a job you are applying for at XYZ Company. In this note you remind him of what your duties were when you worked for him. You also say something about the duties of the position for which you are applying, and how your former duties at ABC Company relate to this new position. This time, if Mr. Jones phones, or if he requests a written letter of recommendation, your former boss, Mr. Rogers, will come across as well-informed about you and about your chances for success on this new job.

As good as this approach has been, there is a still better way to get good job recommendations—one that is used by the most successful job seekers. It is:

Example Three. Write your own letter of recommendation! Believe it or not, people actually do write their own letters of recommendation. I myself have done this on two different occasions. Furthermore, it is perfectly ethical to do this, as long as you do it with the permission of the person you are asking for a recommendation, and as long as you tell the truth about yourself. This third example shows how you can make this happen.

Imagine again that your former boss is sitting in his office. This time, in front of him, is a letter from you, requesting that he be a reference and, along with the letter, a one-page fact sheet, single-spaced, in which you detail exactly how your previous work with his company has demonstrated your qualifications for this new position. You remind him that in August, 1983, when you were working for his company, you were named "Employee of the Month" (he had forgotten that), and how this reflects your effectiveness working with the public, which would be such a major aspect of this new job.

After reading your letter and the accompanying fact sheet, he picks up the phone and dials your number. After complimenting you for your thoroughness in supplying him with the information, he says, "You know, this information you gave me is so complete, it seems silly for me to rewrite it. You seem to know what you want to say about yourself. Why don't you just write it up as if I were saying it, send it on for me to sign, and I'll send it to the person in charge of hiring in the company you are applying to?"

Congratulations! You have just gotten permission to write your own recommendation. Furthermore, you have created a win-win situation for everyone involved. Your former boss has gotten out of having to write a letter. (He has other things to do and, if he is like most of us, he hates writing.) You have gotten yourself an excellent recommendation, written by you. And your new employer has gotten a fantastic new employee—*you*! But this process I am describing only works when the person you are asking for a recommendation knows you very well, *or* when you have given this person information about yourself and your new job so complete that they feel you might just as well write it yourself.

I've Taken Charge of My "Paper Trail." Now What Do I Do?

You now have your "paper" in hand. You have an excellent all-purpose résumé, which you can adapt to a variety of specific job situations. You have several people who are willing to be references, and you have supplied them with enough information—both about your previous work experience and also about the nature of the jobs that you are applying for—that they will be able to do a creditable job. Pretty soon you can expect to hear about one of the positions for which you applied, and you will be asked to come in for an interview. In the next chapter we will give some tips for "surviving the interview."

Chapter Nine

Surviving
the Interview

The prospect of facing a job interview can be a scary experience. But it is the interview that holds the key to actually being offered a job and expressing your vocation by means of paid employment in the world. It is amazing what a good interview can do.

Several years ago I was hiring teachers for a church-related elementary school on the West Coast. I had interviewed several candidates for one position and had, in fact, already decided which of these candidates I was going to hire. Before I had a chance to phone this person, however, I received a call from a woman who introduced herself as an elementary school teacher and said that she had heard we had a position open. She asked if she could come in and interview. Just to be polite, I agreed to see her that very afternoon.

After I hung up, I felt more than a little angry with myself. After all, I had already decided to hire someone else. Why was I seeing this other woman to interview for a position that was already closed? The whole thing seemed like an exercise in futility. Unknown to this woman who was coming in to see me, she had everything going against her: no chance of actually landing the job and, in addition, an angry interviewer who didn't want to see her in the first place!

That afternoon, when she came in, the first thing that struck me was the straightforward and professional manner with which she presented herself. She spoke knowingly of the requirements of working with small children, and her whole attitude reflected a love of teaching and a quiet confidence in her abilities. As I spoke with her, I even found myself wondering whether perhaps I should consider hiring her in place of the other candidate I had already decided upon. Before she left she gave me some local references.

That very afternoon I phoned them. They positively raved about her—"a fantastic teacher . . . a real professional . . . tremendous *rapport* with the kids . . . you'd be fortunate to get her." The end of the story is that I actually *did* hire her for the position, in place of my first candidate, and she turned out to be as excellent as everyone said. I hired her because of her solid work background and also because of her effective interview, which overcame my initial resistance toward her.

Never underestimate the power of a good interview!

Before going into an interview, it is important to have a realistic understanding of just exactly what an interview is, and of what you hope will occur as a result of it. The first step is to realize:

What an Interview Is *Not*

An interview is not Twenty Questions. Twenty Questions is the game where you sit in a chair and answer questions that are thrown at you. If this is what you think the interview is, you're not going to present yourself to your best advantage.

Now to be perfectly honest, there *are* elements of Twenty Questions in an interview. The interviewer *will* ask you questions. And he or she will be expecting you to respond with some of the "right" answers. The problem, however, is that if you think of the interview as Twenty Questions, it will cast you in an overly passive role. None of the real "you" will come across. You may not give the *wrong* answers, but neither will you give the *right* answers. And by right answers I mean simply those answers that convey the person you really are, along with your excitement and enthusiasm about the possibility of being offered this job. In other words, if you step into a Twenty Questions mode, you will not take charge of your interview.

The interview is also not your opportunity to unburden your-self to a wise, older adult. Sometimes individuals who have been out of the job market for some time, or who are somewhat inexperienced as job applicants, may find themselves confiding to an empathetic job interviewer how they have never really done this kind of work before, that their skills may be a little bit rusty, that they realize that their work history isn't really that impressive...

If this might be you, *stop!* Hold everything. The interviewer is not Daddy. He is not your minister or therapist. He is there for one purpose only, and that is to hear how well qualified you are for the position that is being offered.

The interview is not the confessional!

If the interview is not Twenty Questions, and if it is not the confessional—then what is it?

The interview is your opportunity to find out as much as you can about the job being offered and, if you believe the job is right for you, to convince the interviewer that you are the best person for it.

We will now look at the interview process, from your pre-interview preparations up to and including your post-interview follow-up.

Before the Interview

The first thing you need to do is to find out something about the company or organization by which you want to be hired. Why are they in business? What is their product or service? How could you help them *stay* in business, by means of the effective use of your particular skills? Go to your local library. Ask the reference librarian how you could find out more about this company or organization. If you have a friend working in a position similar to the one for which you are applying, ask him or her to tell you something about the nature of his or her duties. The more knowledgeable you are, both about the organization and also about the nature of the job being offered, the more prepared you will be for this interview and the more likely you will be to get the job.

Before the interview, you need also to prepare yourself to answer certain general questions which are often asked. Among these are:

—What are your strengths and weaknesses?
—What are your career goals?
—Why do you believe you are qualified for this position?
—What do you believe you could contribute to this position?

If you haven't thought about questions like these, now is the time to start thinking about them. Formulate some appropriate answers in *advance* of the interview. Try to present your "weaknesses" in a favorable light. An example might be to say, "Sometimes I have a tendency to get too wrapped up in my work." Above all, don't say anything that would seem to suggest that you lack the basic skills, abilities, or temperament to do the job. If you are applying for a job in sales, don't say that your greatest weakness is that you hate relating to people! In general, try to make your answers suggest that you are a person who is well suited for the job, and also one with career goals of your own, and you will strike the interviewer as the kind of competent, purposeful individual that the company or organization wants.

The Day of the Interview

Your first decision is what to wear. Your physical appearance is the "package" you present to the world. It shows the interviewer what you think of yourself and—more important—it gives him or her a clue as to the manner with which you might perform your job responsibilities. In recent years a whole science of clothing has developed, suggesting that people have predictable and measurable emotional responses to different colors and styles of dress.[1] People wearing dark colors, for example, tend to carry more credibility and authority over others. Silly? Of course it is. But if people *do* respond in predictable ways to styles of dress (and the research suggests they do), then it is wise to have your appearance work *for* you instead of *against* you when you come in for your interview. The chart on page 106 shows three different styles of personal appearance, along with the conclusion an interviewer might draw from each. I have chosen for this example a woman, but the general effect would apply equally well to a man.

The first rule in preparing for an interview for any position is to be neat and presentable. Neatness reflects pride in yourself and respect for the interviewer. Second, your clothing and general appearance should reflect contemporary styles without being faddy. This is especially important for those who have been out of the workforce for some time, and for those who have been in the same job for a long time and are now seeking to change jobs, who may have let their appearance slip or not kept up with contempo-

Appearance and Image: Dressing for the Interview

If your appearance is:	*Your interviewer will think:*
a little lacking in neatness, not really "pulled together"	This person needs more pride in herself. Possibly she will take little pride in the job. She may be poor at details. If she comes to work for us we may find that her work is either done poorly or not completed on time.
rather informal and casual, showing no evidence that you have really dressed for the interview	Here is a person who either doesn't *know* what to wear for an interview—in which case she isn't very smart. Or she does know and just doesn't *care*, in which case she is a person who is going to "do her own thing." If she comes to work for us, she is probably going to keep right on doing her thing instead of *our* thing. If we hire this one, we have a real potential for insubordination.
neat, up-to date, and appropriate for the interview	This person has a respect for herself and also a respect for us. She knows how to present herself. She probably brings a professional attitude to her work as well as to her appearance. This one looks like a real winner!

rary styles of dress. Third, dress *up* for the interview. For management and professional or semi-professional level positions, it is a good idea to aim at dressing as well as or better than the interviewer. This means that, if you think your interviewer is likely to be dressed in slacks and a tie and sportcoat, you will want to be dressed at *least* in slacks and a tie and sportcoat (if a man) or, better yet, in a dark navy blue suit. For women a dress or suit should be worn, preferably in subdued colors and fabrics.

If you would like to know more about how your appearance influences other people's attitudes toward you, I recommend the two books by John Malloy mentioned in the chapter footnotes.

During the Interview

Mamie Grossinger, the owner of the famed Grossinger's resort in New York's Catskill Mountains, was fond of saying, "There are no strangers—only friends I haven't met yet." This would be a good attitude to take into your interview. Treat your interviewer as a human being. Smile at him. Make eye contact. Remark on some picture or unusual item in his office, if you feel you can do this without seeming overly familiar. Treat your interviewer as you would treat someone you personally *like,* and the chances are he will like you as well. Someone once said that people tend to hire people that they would feel comfortable going out to lunch with. Human chemistry is important. Make efforts to get it working *for* you during the interview.

As you speak to the interviewer, make an effort to relate your answers to the requirements of the job. It seems too obvious to say, that the *kind* of person you present yourself as being should be "in sync" with the requirements of the position for which you are applying. If, for example, you are applying for a job as a salesman working on commission, don't present yourself as someone who puts a high value on job security. Present yourself instead as one who thrives on challenges and who works most effectively when there are goals to be met. If you are applying for a secretarial position, present yourself as one who is orderly and efficient and who is able to deal effectively working under pressure.

You may discover, during the course of the interview, that the answers you are giving are consistently *out* of sync with the requirements of the position for which you are applying. If, for example, you know that you are *not* orderly and efficient and in fact don't have the slightest interest in *being* orderly and efficient but are instead *wildly* creative, you really have to ask yourself if this position is consistent with the vocation to which God is calling you. If you suspect that this may be the problem, go home after your interview and reread chapter five of this book. Recapture a sense of your real vocation, based on the analysis you did of your interests, values, abilities, and temperament. Figure out exactly *who* you are—and who you *want* to be—before you head out on the interview trail.

During the interview, it is your job to find out as much as you can about the nature of the job being offered, and about what it is like to work for this company. What are the opportunities for advancement? What seems to be the management style of this company? Are employees given freedom to take the initiative, or are they just expected to shut up and do their jobs? These are things you want to know *before* you accept a position working for this company. You will have to judge how much of this you can ask straight out during the interview. To get this information, you may have to "read between the lines" of what the interviewer says and— perhaps more important—what the interviewer *doesn't* say. Even then, you will have to take what he says with the proverbial grain of salt. I remember one job I applied for as an assistant in a church where the senior pastor assured me that his style of operating was democratic, when I just knew, from his manner and his pattern of responding to me, that the opposite was likely to be true. Depending upon how the interview is going, you may have to ask questions of a sensitive nature *after* you receive a firm job offer. However you choose to get the information, just keep in mind that the interview is your opportunity to decide whether *you* want to work for the employers while at the same time they are deciding whether *they* want you to be working *for* them.

After the Interview

You made it through! After the interview you went home, kicked off your shoes, and poured yourself a tall Coke. By now you may have heard whether or not you got the job. If you *did* get it, congratulations! You accomplished your objective, that is, assuming it was the right job for you in the first place.

But what if you didn't get the job?

First off, join the club. You probably were one of several applicants. Only one of them got the job. The old saw, "It's nothing personal," probably applies. It probably wasn't anything "personal" that determined why somebody else got the job and you didn't. It was probably simply that somebody else had better qualifications for that particular job at that particular time than you did. Nothing you could really have done anything about. No reason to run yourself down. Not being offered this particular job does not necessarily mean that God is not calling you to a similar position somewhere else. However, if you can find out exactly *why* this other person got the job—and you didn't—it will be very useful information for you to have in applying for other similar jobs in the future. You need to know, for example, whether you simply lack certain needed qualifications, which you could acquire, or whether, perhaps, you need to present yourself somewhat differently.

If you have been informed that someone else got the position, phone the person who interviewed you. Introduce yourself as someone who interviewed for the job. Thank this person for considering you. Then say, "The position you were offering is almost exactly like the kind of position I am hoping to secure. I was just wondering whether you think there is something else I need in my background in order to be competitive for a position of this nature, or whether there are possibly certain aspects of my previous experience that I should stress—or not stress—in future job interviews." What you are really asking is, "Why didn't I get the job?", but you are asking it in a way that the person becomes your ally in improving your effectiveness as a job candidate. Whatever information this person gives you, treat it like gold! He or she is giving you the key to future employability in the field of your choice.

In any case, it is unlikely that you will be offered a position as a result of your very first interview, or perhaps even your first *few* interviews. It is important, therefore, to adopt an attitude toward your interviews of "practice makes perfect." The more you do, the better you will get. If you average two interviews a day, before long you will become quite comfortable with the process. Author John

Malloy tells of a study he conducted in which he sent professional actors out on job interviews.[2] What he discovered was that the actors were more likely to be offered jobs than people who were actually looking for them. Believe it or not, the implications of this study are actually good news for job seekers. It suggests, first, that if you are at ease in the interview, you are likely to do well. (Those professional actors didn't *need* the job, remember?) And secondly, it suggests that practice *does* make perfect—or at least proficient— and that, like the professional actors, you can learn to be effective in an interview.

Above all, when seeking a position, take the initiative. Be bold. Don't simply send a résumé. Go in person. It is surprising how often people literally walk into a job when they are in "the right place at the right time." As part of the career workshop I attended conducted by Richard Bolles, author of *What Color Is Your Parachute?* Bolles required workshop participants to investigate in person areas of employment that interested them. In introducing this exercise, Bolles remarked how often people in his workshops were offered jobs as a result of doing this exercise—even when they were not seeking jobs in the first place! I myself was once offered a job ahead of thirty names on a waiting list simply because I walked into the employment office the very minute that a worker was needed. Take charge of your situation. Be persistent. Above all, when you *do* interview, see the interview not as an obstacle to be overcome, but rather as your golden opportunity to achieve exactly the job that is right for you.

Chapter Ten

Practical Strategies
That Make a Difference

"All things are possible to him who believes."   —Mark 9:23.

Everyone reading this chapter has a dream. For one it may be starting his own business; for another, changing careers; for still another, landing an excellent position in her present field. Each of these dreams represents a way of living out one's vocation in the world. Whether *you* achieve your dream will probably depend more on the information contained in this chapter than that of any other single chapter in this book. If you follow the suggestions contained in the next few pages, I believe it is highly likely that you will succeed in achieving your dream and living out your true vocation. If you do not follow these suggestions, I believe it is highly likely that you will *not* succeed and that, five years from now, you will still be talking about what you want to do "someday" rather than being well on the way to achieving it. The suggestions contained in this chapter are general principles that have worked for me in accomplishing important goals in my career and in my life and leading me closer to following the path that I believe God has set for me. I feel confident that these suggestions will work for you as well. The first of these is to:

Make Your Goal Your Number One Priority

In chapter five I suggested that you write a goal statement, expressing the nature of the vocation to which you believe God is calling you. If you have not yet written such a goal statement, I suggest that you reread chapter five and write one. Once you have a goal statement that you feel expresses your true vocation, *make achieving your goal your number one priority.* By that I mean, resolve in your own mind, from this time forward, to give first priority in your life to accomplishing those tasks related to achieving your goal, consistently and on a daily basis doing those tasks first, *before* you do the other things you need to do in your life.

When I first started writing this book, I was working seven days a week at three different church positions. For three years, except for vacations, I never had a day off. But I knew, in order to complete this book, which I had set as my number one priority, that I had to make completing it my primary task. Consequently, I set aside forty-five minutes every morning to work on the book. I allowed *nothing* to interfere with this time. One of the jobs I had at this time was editing a monthly newsletter. It would have been tempting to put the book aside while I was struggling to make deadlines on the newsletter. But I had set the book as my number one priority and, by treating it this way, I got the job done!

Do Something Every Day to Achieve Your Goal

Whether your goal is changing jobs, switching careers, or going into business for yourself, this project will involve dozens of separate tasks. People must be phoned, contacts made, applications or forms filled in. Seen all at once, this seems overwhelming. That is why I have found it absolutely essential to commit myself to doing *one thing every day* toward the achievement of the goals I have set for myself. I personally believe that it is this commitment to doing at least one thing every day that is one of the most important predictors of eventual success in the achieving of any goal.

First, let me clarify what I mean by doing one thing every day. I am not talking about the commitment of an hour or two every day. That would be nice, but few of us can afford that kind of commitment. I am talking about one act performed each day toward the achieving of your goal. This one act might be something as simple as looking up a phone number of someone to be contacted the next day. It might take thirty seconds. But it would be the one thing you had done that day to bring your goal that much closer to completion.

"Wait a minute," you say. "If all I've done that day is look up a phone number, and all I'm going to do the next day is actually make the call—why don't I just bunch up a lot of these little tasks and do them all at once on the same day?"

For several reasons. First, there is a cumulative effect of doing many little things over a period of time. It is amazing how much gets done! If the one task you did each day took you an average of five minutes, and you made a point of doing one thing each day for six days out of every week, at the end of each week you would have put in thirty minutes of quality time toward the accomplishment of your goal, to say nothing of a couple of hours spent during the week simply thinking and reflecting about your goal and how best to accomplish it. Second, doing one thing every day insures against procrastination. It would be nice to believe that we would actually *do* these five or six tasks that we have saved up for a free day, but somehow, when that free day comes, we find something else to do and these five or six tasks remain undone. Third, and perhaps most important, doing one thing every day keeps our ultimate goal constantly in front of us. That one task is a constant reminder of our ultimate goal. It makes it harder for us to lose sight of what it is we really want to accomplish.

One final word. When I said, do one thing every day to achieve your goal, I didn't mean literally *every* day. It is important to give yourself time off from pursuing your goal. But this time off should be written into the "contract" you have established with yourself. You might contract with yourself to do one thing every day five days a week, with weekends off. The point is, decide in advance what your "contract" will be, and then stick to it like glue. It will pay off in the achieving of your goal—I guarantee it!

Prepare What You Need to Do in Advance

Setting up the materials you need to complete a task in advance of beginning it is one of the most powerful ways of insuring that you will get the job done when it needs to be done, without delays and without frustrations.

Picture this scene. You are ready to begin writing your résumé. You are sitting at your desk with pencil and paper, ready to start. Suddenly you remember that you don't have the exact dates that you worked for that company back in 1981. Off to the phone you go, to call the company to get the exact dates. Five minutes later you are back at your desk, ready to begin again. Now you realize you can't remember the name of that training course you took during the summer of 1983. Back down to your files you go, to get the name of the course. Back at your desk again, it occurs to you that you don't remember how many academic credits you took during your continuing education back in 1979. By this time you are so hassled and bummed out by this whole thing that you put your résumé aside, to finish on another day. . . .

The situation I describe could have been avoided by preparing the necessary materials in *advance*. That way you would have been mentally and emotionally prepared for writing your résumé, and you would most likely have completed the task on the day you set for it. This general practice of preparing what you need to do in advance applies to all stages of the job-hunt process. For example:

—You are getting ready to set up an informational interview, as described in chapter five. In preparation for this, you write down the name of the person you plan to contact, and the phone number on a pad beside your telephone, where it will be ready for you when you make the call the next day.

—You are preparing to write your résumé, as described in chapter eight. You gather together all your relevant materials and place them on your desk, arranged according to category: educational materials in one pile, information relating to former jobs in another pile, where it will be ready for you to work with when you actually begin to write it the next day.

—You are getting ready for a job interview, as described in chapter nine. The night before, you select the clothes you plan to wear and lay them out on the chair, where they will be ready for you to get into the next morning before you leave for your interview.

Why is it important to prepare what you need to do in advance?

First, it tends to "code your mind" for the task at hand. It allows you to reflect on what you are going to do *before* you do it, and perhaps to consider certain aspects of it that you had not thought of before.

Second, it allows you to deal with any mental resistance you may feel *before* you actually have to do the thing in question. Let's face it—even when you are pursuing a goal of your own choosing, you may have to do things you don't especially enjoy and are not looking forward to. Suppose, for example, you are preparing to set up an informational interview. As your one task for this day, you have decided simply to get the phone number of the person you plan to phone tomorrow. After looking up the number, you experience a lot of mental resistance to actually phoning this person. "I don't even know this guy," you are thinking, "and tomorrow I'm going to phone him up and ask if I can talk to him about his career? This is crazy. He'll never want to see me." This mental resistance that you are experiencing is perfectly normal. It happens to us that ever we face doing something new. But the point is, you want to experience this resistance now—and overcome it—before you actually make this phone call. That way, when you do pick up the phone and dial the number, you will appear confident and in control of yourself.

Use the "Buddy System"

I am indebted to a book by Barbara Sher, entitled *Wishcraft*,[1] for the technique that I will now describe. The Buddy System is simply a way of working with another person for the purpose of achieving goals you mutually set for yourselves. I personally believe that using the Buddy System is second only to the principle of doing one thing every day as a predictor of success in achieving one's goals.

The Buddy System begins with selecting a person you will meet with once a week to work on your goals. This person could be your husband or wife, a friend, or a church member with whom you share similar goals. The first few weeks will likely be spent on clarifying your goals. The following weeks you might concentrate on getting needed information related to achieving your goal or planning the completion of tasks related to your goal. At the same time your friend is helping you work on your goal, you are helping work on your friend's goal. Each week you report on your progress during the previous week and set new goals for the next week. You continue this process until you and your friend have completed the goals you have set for yourselves.

Let me give you an example of how the Buddy System works. Suppose you are considering changing careers. You know that travel has always fascinated you, and you are considering the possibility of working in a travel agency. You have one unresolved question, however. You know you enjoy working directly with people, one-on-one, and you have heard that the modern travel business has become very impersonal and computerized. Your question is, Would a "people person" like me enjoy working in a modern day travel office and, if so, in what capacity? You talk this over with your friend and she and you decide that you need to do some informational interviews with people in the travel business. At the end of the session, you have stated this goal for yourself, "By this time next week, I will know whether a 'people person' like me would be happy working in a modern day travel office." You have also set some specific tasks to achieve your goal, for example, "By this time next week, I will have done at least two informational interviews with people currently working in the travel business." You continue with your friend in this fashion for several weeks—defining goals, specifying tasks to be completed, reporting back and defining still more tasks—until, at the end of several weeks of meeting together, both you and your friend have accomplished the ultimate goals you set for yourselves when you first contracted to meet together.

A word of caution. If you use the Buddy System, your time with your friend is *only* for the discussion of your progress toward reaching your goal. It is *not* a social time. If the person you are meeting with is a personal friend, and you want to spend some time just "visiting" with them, plan enough time to discuss your goals—say, an hour and a half—and then schedule the social visit to begin after that.

The Buddy System is based on the idea that "two heads are better than one." Another person will see things from a slightly different angle. They will tend to see things you have overlooked. They will help to keep you on track. It is easy to put things off when you are operating alone. Another person working alone with you will provide a reality check on your plans, as well as help provide impetus to keep you going, until you have finally achieved your ultimate goal.

Work Your Network

It is said that one-third of all people get their first job because of contacts from family and friends. This fact points out that using network contacts is one of the best ways of landing a job. This is especially true in the case of the estimated eighty percent of all available jobs that are never advertised, that are part of what has been called the "hidden job market." These jobs are typically filled by somebody who knows somebody who knows somebody who knows somebody. If you are one of these "somebodies," you might just get the job!

Where can you look to make contacts to build your network? How about starting with your church? Of the two hundred members, probably *somebody* does the kind of work you are interested in, or at least can steer you to someone who does. Talk to your pastor to find out who this might be. How about people in the clubs you belong to? Friends? Neighbors? Family members? These people are your *network*. Use them to help you achieve your career goals.

Secrets of Success

In this chapter we have looked at various techniques that have been proved to be helpful in enabling people to achieve their goals. Your success in achieving your own personal goals will have much to do with whether or not you actually put these ideas to work. But success also depends upon the kind of mental attitude you direct toward the pursuit of your goal. In the course of my research for this book I was able to identify three "secrets of success" that successful people use to achieve their goals. In the next chapter I will share these with you.

Chapter Eleven

Secrets of Success

"Problems are only opportunities in work clothes."—industrialist Henry J. Kaiser

What is the difference between those who succeed in living out their vocation and those who settle for "just a job"? Why are some people able to take a personal dream and, through effort and ingenuity, make of it a life work, while others never get to first base?

This question was much on my mind as I researched this book, talking to individuals who *had* achieved their dreams, who *were* living out their vocations, as well as others who had possessed dreams but, unlike the others, had never brought them to completion. Why, I wondered, do some succeed while others do not?

As I reflected on this, and as I observed those who *had* the courage to express what they believed to be their vocation, it seemed to me that those who succeed in expressing it possess three characteristics not possessed to the same extent by the others. The first of these characteristics is:

Persistence

Perhaps Calvin Coolidge said it best in these words quoted by Ray Kroc, the founder of McDonald's, in his autobiography, *Grinding It Out* : "Nothing in the world can take the place of persistence. Talent will not; nothing is more common than unsuccessful men with talent. Genius will not; unrewarded genius is almost a proverb. Education will not; the world is full of educated derelicts. Persistence and determination alone are omnipotent."[1]

One thinks of Sigmund Freud, the father of modern psychology, laboring alone in professional obscurity for ten years until other professionals in the field started accepting his ideas. Or inventor Thomas Edison, once consoled by a co-worker for lack of results after several months of failure with his storage battery experiments, who replied, "Why, man, I've got lots of results. I know several thousand things that won't work."[2] Or Walt Disney, who was reputed never to begin work on a new project until at least ten people had first told him that this new project was totally impossible and would never get off the ground.[3] We remember baseball great Babe Ruth as the "Home Run King," but we forget that he also struck out 1,330 times in the course of his career. In the words of San Diego artist and sculptor Tadeusz Lukjanczyk, whom I interviewed for this book, "You've got to accept the grit in your teeth, the marble dust in your sheets, the wood chips on the floor. You must say, 'Well of *course* it's going to be difficult!'"[4]

Those who ultimately succeed have the persistence to plow through whatever obstacles exist, and *get the job done!*

One of the most inspiring stories of persistence that I have ever heard was shared with me by an 86-year-old member of my church in San Diego, California. As a young man newly arrived in this country from his native French-speaking province in Canada, he went to San Diego looking for work. He had been a steelworker in Canada, so he went to the largest shipyard in San Diego seeking employment, and was told there were no positions available. Now this young man was determined he was going to work in that shipyard. In his mind there was no way he was not going to get a job! He politely informed the foreman that he was there to get a job, and that he intended to stay at the gate until a position opened up. The foreman said, in effect, "Be my guest." This conversation occurred on a Monday. On Tuesday morning my friend showed up at the shipyard gate at 7:00 a.m., lunchpail in hand, and stayed until the shift was over. The same on Wednesday. And the same again on Thursday. Later in the day, on Thursday, the foreman called him over.

"Are you really a steelworker?" he asked.

"Yes, I am," my friend replied.

"I'll tell you what," the foreman said. "I'll put you on for this one day on a trial basis. If, at the end of the day, I hear you've done a good job, then you've got a permanent position here. If, on the other hand, I hear you haven't worked out, you'll be gone by the end of the day."

"That's fine with me," my friend replied.

At the end of the day the foreman called over my friend's floor boss. "How's the new guy doing?" he asked.

"That little Frenchman is doing the work of two men," the man replied.

Needless to say, my friend was given a permanent position in the shipyard. Furthermore, the same persistence and determination he had used to get a job he applied to advancing on the job, with the result that, when he retired from that same shipyard forty-two years later, he was supervisor of the entire plant, with direct responsibility for the work of 2,800 men.

The more I reflected on the importance of persistence, such as that shown by my friend, the more I realized that persistence alone did not explain why some people were successful and others were not. There had to be a reason, after all, *why* certain individuals were persistent in the first place. The more I thought about it, the more I realized that, in order to be persistent, a person must first have:

A Clear Sense of Direction

People who are successful in life generally have committed themselves to pursuing one direction at a time, and are consistent in their efforts to express this one direction effectively in their lives. By one direction I mean that they demonstrate a consistent and discernable pattern operating in all the important achievements of their lives. This pattern may be evident in their choice of work, their characteristic style of doing it, or some other identifiable personal trait.

Probably one of the most difficult things in life is to focus on *one* direction and to commit oneself to pursuing this one direction exclusively, to the exclusion of other possibilities that also intrigue one. Scripture warns against being "double-minded" and says that those who are double-minded will not "receive anything from the Lord."[5] It is tempting to avoid the pain of choice by trying to keep all options open. But it is only by choosing that we prepare the way for effective action and eventual success in our chosen endeavor.

My wife and I have friends who, in the six years we knew them, were involved at various times teaching English as a second language in the community college, teaching self-development skills to geriatric patients in a nursing home, planning a program of physical therapy for the disabled, studying real estate investment in hopes of raising the capital to start a counseling center, and attempting to market a friend's invention. At the same time my friend was working part-time as a marriage, family, and child counselor, and completed a doctorate in psychology with a thesis in art therapy. Although there are certain themes that tie together these diverse interests and involvements—for example, an interest in psychology and a desire to help people—nevertheless, I feel my friend was involved in too many *kinds* of activities to do justice to any *one* of them. While this is perhaps an extreme example, most of us are probably somewhat like this in our unwillingness to focus on any one thing. We need to ask ourselves, as my friend might have asked himself, "Who am I *really*? Am I the best teacher of English as a second language in the community? Am I an expert on physical therapy for the disabled? Am I a real estate entrepreneur? Am I a marriage, family and child counselor? Just exactly who is this person called *me*?" The fact is, none of us have the time or energy to do justice to half a dozen completely unrelated occupations and, if we try to do so, we are really saying, "I don't know whether this will work out . . . or this . . . or this . . . so I'd better cover myself by doing them all." What we are really doing is hedging our bets and, consequently, are unable to follow any of these paths fully to success because we have not really committed our time and energies to any one of them. What we must do instead is commit our time and energies to *one* primary path, and then follow this path to its logical conclusion.

How do we achieve this clear sense of direction? Some very few fortunate individuals seem almost to have been born with it. One thinks of the young Picasso, at ten years old already an accomplished artist. Or the successful entrepreneur, at twelve already building up a thriving paper route. Or the future interior decorator, playing with shapes and colors as a young girl. Others seem to arrive at it after many years of trial and error. Suddenly at thirty-seven or forty-three they seem to know exactly what they want to do for the rest of their lives. Most of us, however, do not perceive our natural direction that clearly. At a certain point in our lives, when an increasingly clear sense of direction seems to be emerging, we need to claim it for ourselves and act on it. This involves taking stock of our interests and abilities, our likes and dislikes, and finally saying, "From what I understand about myself at this particular time, the Lord seems to be leading me in *this* direction. Therefore, I will commit myself to pursuing an occupational goal consistent with my vocation as I now understand it."

Persistence is one characteristic of successful people. A clear sense of direction and the willingness to act on it is another. And a third is the articulation of:

Specific Goals

One of the amazing success stories of recent years is the story of the Bethel Bible Series. Headquartered in a multi-million dollar conference center in Madison, Wisconsin, Bethel is the creation of a Lutheran minister named Harley Swiggum, who, more than thirty years ago, was seized by the idea of developing a Bible curriculum for use in churches to help adults study the Bible effectively. The Bethel program is now used in thousands of churches in this country and around the world. When I was in Madison to participate in the Bethel teacher training program, the administrative director of the Bethel foundation, F. Peter Brickman, shared with us one secret of Bethel's success. "The key is not just having goals," Brickman told us. "The key is having *specific* goals."

Think about that for a moment: "The key is not just having goals. It is having *specific* goals."

Successful people are more than goal-oriented. They are oriented to *specific* goals. "I am not a workaholic," remarked one successful businessman quoted in a recent publication, "but I am a goalaholic." The landmark U.S. government study *Work in America* stated this fact: "From biographies of artists, athletes, and successful businessmen, one finds invariably that *these people set goals for themselves.*"[6] This is in spite of the fact that only an estimated two people out of every hundred have set for themselves *specific* goals for what they want to achieve in their lives. If you have set *specific* goals for yourself, you are already ahead of 98 percent of the population!

The key, as I said, is setting *specific* goals. Saying that you would like to be a counselor someday is only a start. In order to make this a *specific* goal, you would have to ask yourself, what would success in this *look* like? A person interested in counseling might say, "Success, for me, would be if, three years from now, I had completed my bachelors degree with a major in counseling from a reputable university, I was employed in a social service agency and was completing my masters degree in counseling at night." Only when we define for ourselves what success in our own particular endeavor would "look like"—for *us*—can we begin to make specific plans to achieve it.

Focus . . . Focus . . . Focus . . . on Your Target

Have you ever marveled at those amazing examples of technological sophistication—those rockets that NASA puts into orbit far above the earth? Do you realize that the Apollo rockets typically are off course 90 percent of the time? It is true! Ninety percent of their inflight time is spent in making a continuing series of mid-course corrections so that they can get back on target again.

Our lives are much like the Apollo rockets. Ninety percent of our time—and probably more!—*we* are "off course." We have lost sight of our own particular target. We are beginning to drift. The important thing at such moments is to make efforts to get back on target again. Success in any endeavor is largely a matter of keeping *your* particular target constantly in your sights and making regular, consistent efforts to attain your goal. The winners in life—those who succeed in doing what *they* want to do, and doing it for the benefit of others—are those who know and follow the three secrets of success: persistence, a clear sense of direction, and having specific goals.

Part Four

Epilogue

Chapter Twelve

The Turtle Road Woods

When you were very young, did you have a "special place"—somewhere you could be yourself and dream about what you wanted to be?

For me that special place was the Turtle Road Woods, an undeveloped tract of land about a mile from our home in Morristown, New Jersey.

I discovered it with a friend one late summer day just before the start of fifth grade. I remember standing on the edge of the woods, smelling the rich moisture from the shaded forest floor, and wondering what mysteries lay concealed in the woods.

The days and weeks that followed were a time of excited exploration, both with my friend and, at other times, alone. First, cautiously, we explored the woods' outer edges. Then, gaining courage, we penetrated farther in. We discovered paths that meandered through the trees, areas of thick growth and areas of meadow clearing, streams, and even an old dike. One day, we peered farther into the woods than we had ever gone before, and it seemed we could make out a huge open area at the center of the forest. What was this open area, we wondered. Was it a meadow? Was it perhaps a lake? We penetrated farther in and discovered it was in fact a lake at the very center of the forest. We spent the rest of that day excitedly exploring its banks. In the days to come we found a raft and pushed out onto the lake, imagining ourselves to be latter-day Tom Sawyers and Huck Finns. The lake became, for us, a special place—a place to share with a friend and also a place to be alone, to experience the silence and solitude of the forest.

Later that year my parents moved to another town. The Turtle Road Woods were left behind. But not the memories of goldenrod on crisp fall days, or of a lake at the heart of the forest.

Many years later, I often found myself thinking about the Turtle Road Woods. I would picture the dark wall of trees as I saw it that first day. I would remember the excitement I felt at peering into the woods and wondering what lay hidden in its deep recesses. Why, I wondered, did that brief period of my life hold such a fascination for me? What was it about the Turtle Road Woods that held my imagination?

One day I suddenly understood my fascination with the woods. The Turtle Road Woods were, for me, a symbol of the process of living and growing. First, there was the discovery of something new. Something exciting. Something *unknown*. After this, the exploration—every day moving farther and farther into uncharted territory. Finally, there was a mystery: What would I find at the center of the forest? What experience awaited me at the end of the journey?

What do the Turtle Road Woods have to do with choosing a career? The woods are a symbol of the process in which you and I are engaged. We too are standing on the edge of the unknown. We are wondering where our explorations will lead. We are trying to find a center for our lives, a place to root our greatest achievements. In one way or another, in whatever clumsy fashion we do it, each of us is trying to find what one writer calls the "innermost core of our being . . . this place where God's will and mine are one and the same."[1] As another writer has said, "The most important discovery we, therefore, can ever make in life is the searching out of what this innermost core of our being tells us is right for us to be doing, what we were created for, what God's plan for our life is . . . and doing what it tells us to do."[2]

It is only when we discover our innermost "core"—and *live* it— that we find not only a *career*. We are finding our true vocation.

Notes

Chapter One

1. The words *underemployed* and *misemployed* seem to be used somewhat interchangeably by writers in the field, although *underemployed* is usually used to refer to an individual working at a position below the level of his or her real abilities, and *misemployed* to one working in the wrong position entirely.
2. The names given in this chapter are fictionalized. The persons portrayed represent composites of many individuals in typical work-related situations.
3. Sheila M. Eby, "When Ambition Comes Out of the Woodwork." *INC.*, September 1982.
4. Charlotte Bühler, "Fulfillment and Failure of Life." *The Course of Human Life*, Charlotte Bühler and Fred Massarik, eds. Springer Publishing Company, 1968, pp. 400 - 403.

Chapter Two

1. Keith Sward, *The Legend of Henry Ford*. Atheneum, 1975.
2. Tennessee Williams quoted by Dotson Rader in "Tennessee Williams." *Parade*, May 17, 1981, p. 16.
3. Matthew Josephson, *Edison*. McGraw-Hill, 1959, p. 45.
4. Abbie Hoffman, "My Life As a Fugitive." *Parade*, December 14, 1980, p. 10.
5. In conversation with the author.
6. Arthur F. Miller and Ralph T. Mattson, *The Truth About You*. Fleming H. Revell, 1977, pp. 50 - 51.

7. C. Tucker, "Henry Moore." *Saturday Review*, March, 1981, p. 46.

8. Richard Corliss, "Steve's Summer Magic." *Time*, May 31, 1982, p. 57.

9. "Ralph Nader," *Current Biography*, Charles Moritz, ed. H. W. Wilson, 1968.

10. Bruce Nichols, "At 73, Famed Heart Surgeon Is Still an Achiever," *The San Diego Union*, October 4, 1981.

11. Sandra Early, "The Cultural Legacy of a Brooklyn Boy," *The San Diego Union*, September 27, 1981.

12. Douglas Bauer, "Because America Never Had a Grandfather," *TV Guide*, March 20, 1982, p. 32 (italics mine).

13. Stafan Kanfer, "The Malady Was Life Itself," *Time*, July 18, 1983, p. 64 (italics mine).

14. Richard Nelson Bolles, *What Color Is Your Parachute?* Ten Speed Press, 1986, p. 95.

15. In conversation with the author.

16. In conversation with the author.

17. Corliss, "Steve's Summer Magic," p. 57.

Chapter Three

1. Isabel Briggs Myers, Report Form for the Myers-Briggs Type Indicator. Palo Alto, CA: Consulting Psychologists Press, 1988. Used by permission of Consulting Psychologists Press.

2. David Keirsey and Marilyn Bates, *Please Understand Me*. Del Mar, CA: Prometheus Nemesis, 1978.

3. Isabel Briggs Myers with Peter B. Myers, *Gifts Differing*. Palo Alto, CA: Consulting Psychologists Press, 1980.

4. Marie-Louise von Franz, "The Inferior Function," *Lectures on Jung's Typology*. Zurich, Switzerland: Spring Publications, 1971, p. 3.

Chapter Four

1. 1 Kings 19:12.
2. Galatians 1:17.
3. I am indebted to several authors in the field of career development and personal growth for the original ideas behind several of the exercises suggested in this chapter. To Richard Nelson Bolles, the presenter of a career development workshop in San Diego, California, October 25-29, 1981, for exercise one, "Things That Really Bug Me About My Job," and exercise three, "Letter to a Friend." To Barbara Sher, with Annie Gottlieb, authors of *Wishcraft: How to Get What You Really Want*, Ballantine, 1983, for exercise two, "The Detective in My House," and exercise five, "Heroes, Mentors, and Role Models," suggested by "The Private Eye Game," pp. 35-37, and "Creating Your Own Cheering Section," pp. 43-45, respectively. To Bernard Haldane, author of *Career Satisfaction and Success*, AMACOM, 1978, for exercise six, "My Greatest Achievements," suggested by his System to Identify Motivated Skills *(SIMS)*, pp. 33-63. And to the Rev. Dr. John Sanford, speaker at the Clergy and Wives Conference of the Episcopal Diocese of San Diego, in Escondido, CA, October 1983, for exercise eight, "Go on a Pilgrimage."
4. Abraham Maslow, *Religions, Values, and Peak-Experiences*. Penguin, 1976; also *Toward a Psychology of Being*, second edition. D. Van Nostrand, 1968, especially chapters six and seven, "Cognition of Being in the Peak-experiences," and "Peak-experiences as Acute Identity Experiences," pp. 71-114.
5. Exodus, chapters 3 and 4.
6. Daniel 2:30.
7. A clearly written guide to understanding your dreams is Ann Faraday's *The Dream Game*. Harper & Row, 1974. See especially the section, "Dream Power as Vocational Counselor," pp. 152-156. For those interested in a religious as well as a psychological point of view, I recommend two books by John A. Sanford: *Dreams and*

Healing. Paulist Press, 1978, and *Dreams: God's Forgotten Language*. Crossroad, 1982, and also a book by Morton Kelsey: *Dreams: A Way to Listen to God*. Paulist Press, 1978.

Chapter Five

1. *Occupational Outlook Handbook*. Washington, D.C.: Department of Labor, revised every two years.
2. *The Dictionary of Occupational Titles*, fourth edition. Washington, D.C.: Superintendent of Public Documents, 1977.
3. The concept of the informational interview was popularized by Richard Nelson Bolles in his best-selling *What Color Is Your Parachute?* Ten Speed Press, occasionally revised.

Chapter Six

1. Nick Canepa, "USUS's Tiny Guard Is Tops with Coach." *San Diego Tribune*, November 13, 1982.
2. *Occupational Outlook Handbook*. Washington, D.C.: Department of Labor, revised every two years.
3. The Career Ability Placement Survey, also known as the CAPS, consists of eight tests administered over a forty minute period, keyed to the abilities needed for eight broad job clusters, representing all the jobs in the United States. Published by Edits/Educational & Industrial Testing Service, P.O. Box 7234, San Diego, CA 92107
4. *Opportunities for College Credit: A CAEL Guide to Colleges and Universities*, available from the Council for Adult and Experiential Learning, 10840 Little Patuxent Parkway, Suite 203, Columbia, MD 21044.
5. Donald M. Dible, author of *Up Your Own Organization! A Handbook on How to Start and Finance a New Business*. Reston, 1981.
6. Information on internships is listed in *The National Directory of Internships*, published by the National Society for Internships and Experiential Education, 3509 Haworth Drive, Suite 207, Raleigh,

NC 27609, and also in *Internships,* published annually by Writer's Digest Books, 1507 Dana Avenue, Cincinnati, OH 45207. These references may be available in the career and placement office of your local college or university.

Chapter Seven

1. Richard Nelson Bolles, in his address at the Four Day Workshop on career development, October 25-29, 1981, in San Diego, CA.
2. "The Itch to Switch Careers." *Changing Times,* July 1982.
3. Jane Clifford, "Surrogate Grandma: It's Scripps Hospital Consultant to the Rescue When New Parents Are Stuck for an Answer." *San Diego Union,* December 28, 1983.
4. John C. Crystal and Richard N. Bolles, *Where Do I Go from Here with My Life?* Ten Speed Press, 1974, p. 134.
5. "New Dreams Are Built on Corporate Cutbacks." *Standard Times,* New Bedford, MA, August 3, 1986, reprinted from *Wall Street Journal - ONS.*
6. Alfred E. Osborne, Jr., "Taking the Plunge." *Black Enterprise,* October, 1982, p. 34.
7. John Naisbitt, *Megatrend.* Warner Books, 1984, p. 160.
8. "Nation's Self-employed Ranks Expanding." *San Diego Tribune,* August 8, 1984.
9. "Americans Volunteer, 1985," a survey done by the Gallop organization for Independent Sector, reported by the Volunteer National Center, 1111 North 19th Street, Suite 500, Arlington, VA 22209.

Chapter Nine

1. John T. Malloy, *Dress for Success.* Warner Books, 1975. For women, Malloy has written *The Woman's Dress for Success Book.* Warner Books, 1978.
2. John T. Malloy, *Malloy's Live for Success.* Bantam Books, 1983, p. 70.

Chapter Ten

1. Barbara Sher, with Annie Gottlieb, *Wishcraft: How to Get What You Really Want.* Ballantine, 1979, p. 227.

Chapter Eleven

1. Ray A. Kroc, *Grinding It Out.* St, Martin's Press, 1987, p. 201.

2. Quoted by Ray Stannard Baker in "Edison's Latest Marvel," *Windsor Magazine,* November 1902. Cited by Matthew Josephson in *Edison.* McGraw Hill, 1959, p. 413.

3. Denis Waitley, *Seeds of Greatness: The Ten Best-Kept Secrets of Total Success.* Pocket Books, 1984, p. 42.

4. Personal conversation with the author.

5. James 1:8.

6. *Work in America: Report of a Special Task Force to the Secretary of Health, Education and Welfare.* The MIT Press, 1973, p. 50, (italics mine).

Chapter Twelve

1. Mary Michael, "Source, Guide and Goal." *The Living Church,* June 28, 1981, p. 11.

2. H. A. Williams, *True Christianity.* Templegate, 1975. Cited by Mary Michael, *Ibid.,* p. 11.

Resource Guide

Selected Bibliography

There are a large number of books available on virtually every aspect of choosing and implementing a career. The problem is one of selection. I make no claim that the books listed here are necessarily the "best." They are, however, in most cases, books that I have used myself and found helpful, and that I believe would be helpful to the general reader. I have listed the latest edition available for each.

Basic Reference

Occupational Outlook Handbook. Washington, DC: U.S. Department of Labor, revised every two years. A description of two hundred occupations employing well over half of all the jobs in the United States, arranged according to clusters of related occupations. Available in the reference section of your local library, or by order from: Superintendent of Documents, U.S. Government Printing Office, Washington, DC, 20402. This is one you might want to buy for yourself, especially if you feel you will be exploring several different career possibilities over a period of time.

The Dictionary of Occupational Titles, fourth edition. Washington, DC: Superintendent of Public Documents, 1977. The "bible" of vocational information, the *D.O.T.* contains twenty thousand job titles. If you can't find the particular job you are interested in in the *Occupational Outlook Handbook,* above, you will most likely find it in the *D.O.T.* The *D.O.T.* lists more jobs, but with less detailed information on each. There is no need to buy this one for yourself. Simply refer to it when needed in the reference section of your local library.

General Interest

Richard Nelson Bolles, *What Color Is Your Parachute?* Ten Speed Press, occasionally revised. Probably the best-known and best-selling book in the career development field. Especially noteworthy for its easy-to-read and lighthearted (yet essentially serious) approach and for its exhaustive compendium of career-related resources in the appendix. Another standard in the field is Bernard Haldane's *Career Satisfaction and Success.* AMACOM, 1982. Haldane's book contains his "System to Identify Motivated Skills (SIMS)," a method of identifying personal interests and values in preparation for making job and/or career decisions. Another book in a similar vein is Arthur F. Miller and Ralph T. Mattson, *The Truth About You.* Fleming H. Revell, 1977.

Two books that concentrate less on self-assessment and more on the demands of the job-hunt are: Richard Germann and Peter Arnold, *Bernard Haldane Associates' Job and Career Building.* Ten Speed Press, 1982. Richard K. Irish, *Go Hire Yourself an Employer.* (Anchor) Doubleday, 1978.

Finally, if you would like to indulge in a little financial voyerism (and who among us wouldn't!) I recommend David Harrop's *Paychecks: Who Makes What?* Harper Colophon, 1980. Another is Gerald Krefetz and Philip Gittelman's *The Book of Incomes.* Holt, Rinehart and Winston, 1982. Most of this same financial information is available, updated, in the U.S. government-published *Occupational Outlook Handbook.*

Career Choice and Personality Type

To explore how personality type affects career choice, I recommend *Please Understand Me*, by David Keirsey and Marilyn Bates, containing the "Keirsey Temperament Sorter," a self-scoring version of the "Myers Briggs Types Indicator," a questionnaire designed to assist you in assessing your personality type. Prometheus Nemesis, 1978. Another is *Gifts Differing*, by Isabel Briggs Myers with Peter B. Myers. Consulting Psychologists Press, 1980.

John Holland's studies on the relation of work environment to personality type are summarized in a paperback entitled *If You Don't Know Where You're Going, You'll Probably End Up Somewhere*

Else, by David P. Campbell. Argus, 1974. Holland's theory is also the basis for Richard Nelson Bolles' "The quick job-hunting map" in *What Color Is Your Parachute?.*

Motivation and Goal Setting

The best book I know for transforming a wish into a reality, one step at a time, is *Wishcraft: How to Get What You Really Want,* by Barbara Sher with Annie Gottlieb. Ballantine, 1983. A book that tells how to *Know What You Want: And Get It!* is by Norman Monath. Cornerstone, 1984. Denis Waitley and Reni L. Witt emphasize the importance of incorporating a life goal into one's work in *The Joy of Working.* Dodd, Mead, 1985.

Time Management

A clear, simple guide to managing time and establishing personal priorities is *How to Get Control of Your Time and Your Life,* by Alan Lakein. (Signet) New American Library, 1974. Lakein identifies common time wasters and suggests practical strategies for overcoming them.

Résumés

Yana Parker, in *The Damn Good Resume Guide,* shows how to write a brief, focused, and effective résumé, relating one's work history, education, and training directly to one's job objective. Ten Speed Press, 1986.

Personal Appearance

John T. Malloy's *Dress for Success* discusses clothes and personal appearance and their effect on how people perceive you. Warner Books, 1976. A companion volume is *The Woman's Dress for Success Book.* Warner Books, 1978. This same author takes a broader perspective, looking not only at clothes but also at body language and speech patterns, in *Malloy's Live for Success.* Bantam Books, 1983. You may not like what Malloy has to say, but you can't ignore it either!

Interviewing

Perhaps the best single book on interviewing is *Sweaty Palms: The Neglected Art of Being Interviewed,* by H. Anthony Medley. Ten Speed Press, 1984. Also recommended is *How to Turn an Interview into a Job,* by Jeffrey G. Allen. Simon and Schuster, 1983. Allen suggests practical strategies for taking the lead in lining up job interviews and turning those interviews into firm job offers.

For Women

Catalyst, the national women's career organization, has produced *What to Do with the Rest of Your Life.* (Touchstone) Simon and Schuster, 1981. *What to Do . . .* discusses how to define skills and set personal goals, and describes women's opportunities in a variety of fields, from health care to business.

For Young People

For young people who want to start thinking about choosing a career, as well as for adults who want a good introduction to some important career-related topics, I recommend three books by David P. Campbell, the co-author of the "Strong-Campbell Interest Inventory." They are, on goal setting: *If You Don't Know Where You're Going, You'll Probably End Up Somewhere Else.* Argus, 1974. On developing your creative potential: *Take the Road to Creativity and Get Off Your Dead End.* Argus, 1977. On developing leadership qualities: *If I'm in Charge Here Why Is Everybody Laughing?* Center for Creative Leadership, 1984.

For Liberal Arts Graduates

For philosophy, literature, and other liberal arts graduates who wonder if there is life after academia, Dorothy K. Bester explores career opportunities from editing to self-employment in *Aside from Teaching, What in the World Can You Do? Career Strategies for Liberal Arts Graduates*. University of Washington Press, 1982.

Self-Employment

A good introduction to the topic (and not just for students) is Brett M. Kingstone's *The Student Entrepreneur's Guide*. Ten Speed Press, 1981. If you are hooked on the idea of self-employment and would like to explore the possibility in more depth, I recommend Donald M. Dible's *Up Your Own Organization! A Handbook on How to Start and Finance a New Business*. Reston, 1981.

Alternative Work Styles

If you are turned on by the idea of doing your own thing in your own way and getting paid for it, I recommend *Working Free: Practical Alternatives to the Nine to Five Job*, by John Applegath. AMACOM, 1982. A practical and detailed guide to successful free-lancing is *The Free-lance Writer's Survival Manual*, by Ernest E. Mau. Contemporary Books, 1981. Many of the procedures described in Mau's book could be applied to free-lancing in fields other than writing.

From a Spiritual Perspective

Surprisingly little has been written from a spiritual perspective on choosing and implementing a life work. One is *Finding a Job You Can Love*, by Ralph Mattson and Arthur Miller. Thomas Nelson,

1983. Mattson and Miller look at work not only as a way to make a living but also as an opportunity to make the best use of the abilities that God has given one. Two books that look at work from the perspective of finding one's identity as a person are *Making a Life: Career, Commitment and the Life Process*, by Gene Ruyle. Seabury, 1983, and *Do What You Love, the Money Will Follow*. Paulist Press, 1988. For women, Nancy van Vuuren has written *Work and Career*. The Westminster Press, 1983.